Manual of

Nursing Diagnosis

ELEVENTH EDITION

Including all diagnostic categories approved by the
North American Nursing Diagnosis Association

Marjory Gordon, PhD, RN, FAAN
Professor of Nursing (Emeritus)
Boston College
Chestnut Hill, Massachusetts

JONES AND BARTLETT PUBLISHERS
Sudbury, Massachusetts
BOSTON   TORONTO   LONDON   SINGAPORE

World Headquarters
Jones and Bartlett Publishers
40 Tall Pine Drive
Sudbury, MA 01776
978-443-5000
info@jbpub.com
www.jbpub.com

Jones and Bartlett Publishers Canada
6339 Ormindale Way
Mississauga, Ontario L5V 1J2
CANADA

Jones and Bartlett Publishers International
Barb House, Barb Mews
London W6 7PA
UK

Jones and Bartlett's books and products are available through most book-
stores and online booksellers. To contact Jones and Bartlett Publishers
directly, call 800-832-0034, fax 978-443-8000, or visit our website,
www.jbpub.com.

Substantial discounts on bulk quantities of Jones and Bartlett's publica-
tions are available to corporations, professional associations, and other
qualified organizations. For details and specific discount information,
contact the special sales department at Jones and Bartlett via the above
contact information or send an email to specialsales@jbpub.com.

ISBN-13: 978-0-7637-4045-0
ISBN-10: 0-7637-4045-4
ISSN: 0748-920X
6048

Production Credits
Acquisitions Editor: Kevin Sullivan
Production Director: Amy Rose
Associate Editor: Amy Sibley
Associate Production Editor: Alison Meier
Senior Marketing Manager: Emily Ekle
Manufacturing Buyer: Amy Bacus
International Consultant: Juergen Georg
Composition: ATLIS Graphics
Cover Design: Kristin E. Ohlin
Printing and Binding: United Graphics
Cover Printing: United Graphics

Printed in the United States of America
10 09 08 07 06   10 9 8 7 6 5 4 3 2 1

Contents

Preface

This is the 11th edition of the *Manual of Nursing Diagnosis*. Since 1982 when the first edition of this manual was published, there have been many changes in health care. All the changes support the need for a language to communicate nursing practice. In particular, documentation in the computerized patient record requires clear, concise nursing diagnoses and a handy reference manual to support diagnostic judgments. Ten previous editions underscore the fact that nurses find the nursing diagnoses useful in describing their clinical judgments about health-related conditions, projecting outcomes, and planning interventions.

The organization of the diagnoses in this manual within the functional health patterns framework facilitates assessment and diagnosis. Clinical usefulness of this framework and organization of the diagnoses has been demonstrated both nationally and internationally by the wide use of this manual. The patterns are relevant across cultures, nursing specialties, age groups, and levels of acuity. Individuals, families, and communities can be assessed and problems and strengths identified.

Functional health patterns provide an easily learned framework for assessment and critical thinking within the clinical judgment process. Assessment guidelines and diagnoses are grouped under the same categories. This consistency facilitates the movement from assessment data to nursing diagnosis.

"Without a language, nursing is invisible." These words are contained in a document published by the International Council of Nurses.[1] Without a diagnostic language, professional practice is reduced to a description of tasks used in intervention and standardized outcomes that disregard the individuality of persons and human responses.

The *Manual of Nursing Diagnosis, Eleventh Edition,* contains the evolving diagnostic language of professional nursing. It has new nursing diagnoses that are in the process of being developed, incorporates research on diagnostic categories, and has features to facilitate students' and nurses' critical thinking and diagnostic judgment.

One of the most important features for users of the manual is the identification of diagnostic cues for a great number of nursing diagnoses. Diagnostic cues are the criteria for making a judgment. Diagnostic cues perform the following functions:

+ Are few in number but critical for diagnostic judgment
+ Increase reliability, consistency, and accuracy in diagnosis
+ Help distinguish among diagnoses
+ Focus assessment, making the judgment process more efficient
+ Discourage labeling of behavior without sufficient data

Another useful feature of many diagnoses in this edition is the listing of high-risk populations of clients. This feature can be used to increase sensitivity to the condition during an assessment, as explained in the section, "Use of Diagnostic Categories in Clinical Practice." Previously, some high-risk populations were hidden among the defining characteristics.

Finally, included in this edition are the following:

+ Seventeen new diagnoses approved at the national conference of the North American Nursing Diagnosis Association (NANDA) International
+ Multiple revisions of diagnoses approved by NANDA International, and 26 additional diagnoses developed by the author that are useful in clinical practice but not yet reviewed by NANDA International

PREFACE

As in the past, this manual provides a quick pocket reference and is useful for learners and expert diagnosticians. Learners will be interested in the concise terms used to describe a cluster of signs and symptoms exhibited by the client and the functional health pattern guidelines for assessment and diagnosis. Experts can get information quickly by accessing nursing diagnoses in various ways. Each diagnosis is clearly presented beginning on a new page. Blank pages are provided following each pattern area for personal notes about important observations, interventions, outcomes, or other learning.

Sample admission assessment guides are included for the family, community, and individual (adults, infants, young children, and critical care clients). Sections on how diagnoses can be used to guide questions and observations beyond the basic assessment and how to use diagnostic categories in other clinical activities (e.g., critical paths, quality improvement) provide a quick reference. Professional documentation is stressed and is illustrated using the problem-oriented format.

This 11th edition of the *Manual of Nursing Diagnosis* is organized to meet the needs of both novices and expert diagnosticians. Because of interest in the health patterns and nursing diagnoses, a bibliography on use of functional patterns is included (pages 5 to 8). The increasing use of nursing diagnoses by students and graduate nurses around the world is indicated by the fact that the *Manual of Nursing Diagnosis* has been translated into Japanese, Chinese, Swedish, Finnish, Dutch, German, Italian, Spanish, Slovenian, and French. It is hoped that this 11th edition will be equally well received both in North America and throughout the world of professional nursing practice.

Acknowledgments

Most of the diagnostic categories contained in this manual are based on the work of NANDA International as published in *Nursing Diagnoses: Definitions and Classification, 2005–2006.** This reference should be consulted for research and reviews; the *Manual of Nursing Diagnosis* is specifically designed for clinical practice. The diagnosis of parent-infant separation was suggested to the author by T. Heather Herdman, PhD, RN, Clinical Nurse Specialist, based on her research in neonatal intensive care.

Marjory Gordon

Publisher's Acknowledgment:

The publisher would like to thank Juergen Georg of Verlag Hans Huber Publishing in Bern, Switzerland for his assistance with bringing the 11th edition of this work to fruition.

Use of the Manual

A diagnostic manual can serve many purposes. For students, it is a quick reference during clinical practice, a useful guide in class or clinical conference, and a necessity for doing homework. For expert diagnosticians, it is a clinical reference, a research tool, a teaching or management resource, and a stimulus for ideas. For both learners and experts, it is a much-used companion.

This manual contains the most up-to-date diagnostic categories contained in the NANDA International Diagnostic Taxonomy. This taxonomy is endorsed by the American Nurses Association and included in the International Classification for Nursing Practice. Diagnostic terms, definitions of terms, defining characteristics (risk factors for high-risk diagnoses) are included, as are etiological/related factors and high-risk populations for actual diagnoses.

The manual has eight main uses that support clinical judgment in nursing practice:

Access to nursing diagnoses—It is a quick reference to terms used in formulating nursing diagnoses.

Use of diagnostic terms—Each nursing diagnosis term in the manual describes a condition of concern to nurses. The diagnostic term stands for a concept that explains the meaning of a set of cues. As with any terms in a language, each has a standard definition and characteristics. It is the speaker or writer's responsibility to use the terms correctly. Internationally, nurses are working toward a uniform nursing language and an international classification system of nursing diagnoses.

Criteria for diagnostic judgments—When nursing or other research is available, diagnostic cues are specified. In conjunction with supporting data, these may be used as criteria for making the diagnosis.

Functional health pattern assessment guidelines: Data to diagnosis—Guides are included for linking assessment and diagnosis using functional health patterns and diagnostic groupings in the index. In many instances the client's problem can be formulated by using one diagnostic category to describe the problem and another category from the same, or a different, functional pattern area to describe etiological factors. Risk factors may be in multiple pattern areas.

High-risk populations—Some of the conditions described by nursing diagnoses are prevalent in certain groups of people in certain situations or having particular experiences or treatments. High-risk populations of clients/persons are listed in the manual for some diagnoses in which incidence is fairly well established.

Diagnosis-specific treatment—Formats for diagnosis-specific treatment plans are outlined.

Documentation—Format, guidelines, and examples of documentation are provided.

Special notes—Pages are included for special notes following each pattern area. Using this manual for each of these purposes is discussed below.

Access to Nursing Diagnoses

Different situations require different ways of accessing nursing diagnoses. The manual can accommodate the following needs:

  ♦ To find a diagnostic category to describe a cluster of signs and symptoms within a functional pattern area, use the Diagnostic Categories on pages xxi to xxviii.

Diagnoses are grouped by functional patterns. Each diagnosis is clearly presented on its own page.

+ When a diagnostic category label is known but you need to check the definition, diagnostic or supporting cues, or etiological/related factors, use the Alphabetical Index to look up the page number. The Alphabetical Index serves as a dictionary of diagnostic terms *(pages 387 to 398 and inside covers)*.
+ If you wish to scan all the diagnostic categories within a particular functional pattern area, use the Contents on *pages xxi to xxviii* as an index to the pattern.
+ For research on NANDA-accepted diagnostic categories, use diagnostic categories in *NANDA Nursing Diagnoses: Definitions and Classification, 2005–2006.*[2]

Use of Diagnostic Terms

The diagnostic categories contained in this manual are concepts used in thinking, and they represent a language for communicating. They are used to describe professional nurses' diagnostic judgments about actual or potential health problems and health related conditions. A useful nursing diagnosis statement consists of terms describing (1) the problem or condition and (2) the primary etiological or related factor(s) contributing to the problem or condition that is the focus of nursing treatment.

Many types of judgments are made in practice, but the term *nursing diagnosis* is reserved for client conditions that "nurses by virtue of their education and experience are capable and licensed to treat."[3] NANDA International's definition of a nursing diagnosis further clarifies the term:

A nursing diagnosis is a clinical judgment about an individual, family, or community response to actual or potential health problems/life processes which provides the basis for definitive therapy toward achievement of outcomes for which the nurse is accountable.[2]

This builds on a definition based on Shoemaker's research that integrates nursing diagnosis into nursing process:

> Nursing diagnosis is a clinical judgment about an individual, family, or community that is derived through a deliberate, systematic process of data collection and analysis. It provides the basis for prescriptions for definitive therapy for which the nurse is accountable. It is expressed concisely and includes the etiology of the condition when known.[4]

Nursing diagnoses are primarily resolved by nursing care methods, and nurses assume accountability in practice for treatment outcomes. If a diagnosis does not meet these criteria, a notation to refer the problem for medical evaluation will be found on the page containing the diagnosis. An additional characteristic that distinguishes nursing diagnoses is that professional nurses assume responsibility for research on the conditions.

Nurses view the diagnostic categories in this manual from various conceptual perspectives. Depending on the model of nursing used to guide the nursing process and practice, diagnoses may be viewed as self-care agency deficits, ineffective adaptations, human response patterns, needs, or simply dysfunctional health patterns. There is no consensus on the conceptual focus of nursing and thus no consensus on the focus of nursing diagnosis.

Users of the manual should recognize that nursing diagnoses are in the process of development, especially the 26 diagnoses in this manual that are formally under development. Diagnostic categories require conceptual work and further clinical study. It is expected that nurses will modify, delete, and add to the currently accepted classifications. Revisions will occur as diagnoses are used (1) to organize assessment data, (2) as a basis for care planning, and (3) as a focus for nursing documentation. Nurses are encouraged to submit refinements of diagnoses to NANDA International. Diagnoses are reviewed at various levels of development, from just a label and definition to being supported by clinical research. Descriptions of these levels and the process for submission and review can be obtained on the NANDA International Web site.

All diagnostic categories contain the following components: diagnostic category label, definition, defining characteristics (diagnostic and supporting cues), and for actual problems, etiological or related factors. Risk conditions or potential problems have risk factors instead of defining characteristics and etiological factors. Healthy states or processes may have supporting factors rather than etiological/related factors.

Defining characteristics and risk factors are the observations used to make a diagnostic judgment about the presence or absence of a condition. In the manual, defining characteristics are presented as (1) diagnostic cues and (2) supporting cues. Current research evidence suggests that diagnostic cues are the most valid and reliable indicators for diagnosing the condition. Supporting cues used in conjunction with diagnostic cues increase psychological confidence in diagnostic judgments. These cues generally capture variations in behavior across populations and situations. Supporting cues are not specific to one diagnosis; during assessment they may suggest a few diagnoses. Usually confidence in a diagnostic judgment is attained with the use of the diagnostic cues and some supporting data.

Recommendations of diagnostic and supporting cues in this manual are based on (1) review of research on nursing diagnoses published in NANDA International conference proceedings and in *International Journal of Nursing Terminologies and Classification*), (2) the author's pooled research data from national studies using 1100 experts in critical care, rehabilitation, and home care nursing, (3) literature from other disciplines and nursing textbooks when research was minimal or absent, and (4) the author's judgment and logical analysis in the context of diagnostic reasoning and parsimony. For example, if tissue destruction and traumatized tissue are listed, parsimony dictates that the cue, broken skin, is redundant. In a few cases in which diagnoses were not specific (broad taxonomic categories), no recommendation was made. Risk factors may vary with the client population, and insufficient research exists on various populations.

Meta-analyses, integrated research reviews of each diagnosis, concept analysis, and further analyses of data will serve to test the usability of these criteria and the validity of the ratings and diagnostic cues. Nursing research is insufficient for many diagnoses, and in many cases, no replications of large studies exist. In particular, there are minimal studies on possible differences among age and cultural groups. These factors should be kept in mind when using the diagnostic and supporting cues.

The diagnostic cues are used to determine if the condition described by the diagnosis is present or not present. Also, these cues can be used for differential diagnosis among conditions and, most importantly, to justify a diagnostic judgment. For most diagnoses describing a subjective state, diagnostic cues need to include both observation and verbal report.

Clinical experience has demonstrated that the assessment database and the judgment of the nurse determine whether a diagnostic category is used as a probable cause (etiological or related factor) or to describe a problem in the diagnostic statement. *Use the nursing diagnoses in the manual as a dictionary of terms and concepts.* For some diagnoses a footnote suggests that the diagnosis is frequently the *focus* for intervention (i.e., frequently used as an etiological/related factor). In these cases, it is the probable cause of other problems.

Functional Health Pattern Assessment: Data to Diagnosis

The manual contains an assessment format and diagnostic groupings that facilitate the move from data to diagnosis. Both employ the functional health patterns as a nursing perspective on individual, family, and community health care. It is possible that cognitive strain and diagnostic errors can be reduced if there is consistency between organization of assessment data and grouping of diagnostic categories. For example, if data on the client's elimination pattern can be compared to defining characteristics of diagnoses in the elimination pattern, less effort is required than when using an unorganized database and a very large number of alphabetized diagnoses. The following are guidelines for use of the manual in the diagnostic phase of nursing process:

1. Use the manual both to learn the 11 functional health patterns and to study the diagnostic categories commonly occurring in your practice area. Functional patterns are an easily learned nursing model for assessment. Review the diagram on Components of Nursing Process, pages 40–41, to place nursing diagnosis in the context of nursing process and clinical judgment.

2. Use the assessment guidelines (pages 10–35) that are based on the functional health pattern areas (pages 2–5) to collect and organize a nursing history and examination of adults (pages 11–16), adults in critical care (pages 32–35), infants and young children (pages 16–21), families (pages 21–25), or communities (pages 26–31). Also contained in the manual is a bibliography of articles on the use of functional health patterns in clinical activities (pages 5–8).

3. If assessment reveals a dysfunctional pattern but the name escapes you, check the diagnoses listed under the pattern (Diagnostic Categories, pages 57–379) for terminology

to label the condition. Use the defining characteristics listed with each diagnosis to validate your judgment. Etiological or risk factors listed with each diagnosis may suggest possible reasons for the problem or risk state.

4. For a quick reference before documenting a problem, use either the Diagnostic Categories (pages xxi–xxviii), the Alphabetical Index (pages 387–398 and inside covers), or the quick reference to diagnostic categories (outside back cover). Turn to the page corresponding to the possible diagnostic label. Check that the observed signs and symptoms correspond to the defining characteristics of the diagnostic category, particularly the suggested diagnostic cues.

High-Risk Populations

Statistics suggest that some conditions described by nursing diagnoses are prevalent in certain groups of people, in certain situations, or during certain experiences or treatments. For example, the population of persons with a stroke and impaired bed mobility are at high risk for pressure ulcer, and elderly persons living alone with reduced social contacts are prone to depression. The base rate of occurrence is high. Knowing this, clinicians are sensitive to cues during assessment (and exercise caution that statistical incidence of a condition does not affect judgment more than clinical data). Early case finding is due in part to a sensitivity to cues.

In the manual, high-risk populations are listed for some diagnoses in which incidence is fairly well established. Use this information as a basis for raising the possibility that a condition may be present when doing an assessment. Add your own observations to the notes pages that follow each pattern area.

Diagnosis-Specific Treatment/Intervention

A nursing diagnosis is used as a basis for projecting out-comes, planning interventions, and evaluating outcome at-tainment. The problem statement is the basis for outcome projection, that is, the identification of behaviors that signify resolution of the problem. These projected outcomes are then used to document progress toward outcome attainment and to evaluate resolution of the problem.

The etiological factor(s) are the focus for designing inter-ventions that will reduce or eliminate the factors contribut-ing to the problem.[5] Outcome attainment is the measure of effectiveness of the intervention. In the case of a potential or high-risk problem, reduction or elimination of risk factors is the desired outcome.

Documentation

The Problem-Oriented Recording Format Guidelines and Checkpoints (pages 47–49) will be useful in ensuring consis-tency between the nursing diagnosis, the projected outcome, and the intervention plan. An example is provided (pages 49–56).

Documentation is important for statistical purposes. Cur-rently a nursing minimum data set (NMDS) is being studied in a number of countries. This requires documentation of nursing diagnoses, interventions, and outcomes. The NMDS also includes an acuity factor.[6]

Special Notes

It is important to learn from practice, rather than just practic-ing! One of the ways to continue learning is to develop the habit of reflecting on insights and new information, creative interventions, or cost-effective methods. Pages following each pattern area labeled *NOTES* are valuable for recording clinical information related to each diagnosis such as important additional cues or etiological factors that have been observed, factors related to a specific population of clients, and interventions that are successful in reaching projected outcomes.

References

1. International Council of Nurses. *Nursing's Next Advance: Classification for Nursing Practice.* Geneva, Switzerland: International Council of Nurses; 1994.
2. NANDA International. *Nursing Diagnoses: Definitions and Classification, 2005-2006.* Philadelphia, PA: NANDA International; 2005.
3. Gordon M. Nursing diagnosis and the diagnostic process. *Am J Nurs.* 1976;76:1276–1300.
4. Shoemaker J. Essential features of a nursing diagnosis. In Kim MJ, McFarland GK, McLane AM, eds. *Classification of Nursing Diagnoses: Proceedings of the Fifth National Conference.* St Louis, MO: Mosby; 1984.
5. McCloskey J, Bulechek GM. *Nursing Interventions Classification (NIC).* St Louis, MO: Mosby-Elsevier; 2004.
6. Werley H, Lang N. Identification of the Nursing Minimum Data Set. New York, NY: Springer; 1988.

Notice

The authors, editor, and publisher have made every effort to provide accurate information. However, they are not responsible for errors, omissions, or for any outcomes related to the use of the contents of this book and take no responsibility for the use of the products described. Research, clinical practice, and government regulations often change the accepted standard in this field. In the clinical setting, the health care provider or reader is responsible for determining the appropriate usage of nursing process and its terminology.

Diagnostic Categories

Boldface type indicates diagnoses currently accepted by NANDA International (North American Nursing Diagnosis Association). Others are diagnoses developed by the author, not yet reviewed by this association, but are found to be useful in clinical practice. See inside front and back covers for diagnoses arranged in alphabetical order.

Health-Perception–Health-Management Pattern

DIAGNOSTIC CATEGORIES

Nutritional-Metabolic Pattern

DIAGNOSTIC CATEGORIES

Elimination Pattern

DIAGNOSTIC CATEGORIES

Activity-Exercise Pattern

DIAGNOSTIC CATEGORIES

Self-Perception–Self-Concept Pattern

Role-Relationship Pattern

DIAGNOSTIC CATEGORIES

Sexuality-Reproductive Pattern

Coping–Stress-Tolerance Pattern

DIAGNOSTIC CATEGORIES

Value-Belief Pattern

Functional Health Patterns Typology

This section contains a typology of health patterns and their definitions, which are used for organizing assessment and grouping nursing diagnoses.

TYPOLOGY

Functional health patterns of clients, whether individuals, families, or communities, evolve from client-environment interaction. Each pattern is an expression of biopsychosocial integration, thus no one pattern can be understood without knowledge of the other patterns.

Functional patterns are influenced by biological, developmental, cultural, social, and spiritual factors. Dysfunctional health patterns (described by nursing diagnoses) may occur with disease; dysfunctional health patterns may also lead to disease.

The judgment of whether a pattern is functional or dysfunctional is made by comparing assessment data to one or more of the following: (1) individual baselines, (2) established norms for age-groups, or (3) cultural, social, or other norms. A particular pattern has to be evaluated in the context of other patterns and its contribution to optimal function of the client. Definitions of patterns are listed below.

1 HEALTH-PERCEPTION–HEALTH-MANAGEMENT PATTERN

Describes the client's perceived pattern of health and well-being and how health is managed. Includes the individual's perception of health status and its relevance to current activities and future planning. Also included is the individual's health-risk management and general health-care behavior, such as safety practices and adherence to mental and physical health promotion activities, medical or nursing prescriptions, and follow-up care.

2 NUTRITIONAL-METABOLIC PATTERN

Describes pattern of food and fluid consumption relative to metabolic need and pattern indicators of local nutrient supply. Includes the individual's patterns of food and fluid consumption: daily eating times, the types and quantity of food and fluids consumed, particular food preferences, and the use of nutrient or vitamin supplements. Describes breastfeeding and infant feeding patterns. Includes reports of any skin lesions, ability to heal, and measures of body temperature, height, and weight. General appearance of well-being and condition of skin, hair, nails, mucous membranes, and teeth are included.

3 ELIMINATION PATTERN

Describes patterns of excretory function (bowel, bladder, and skin). Includes the individual's perceived regularity of excretory function, use of routines or laxatives for bowel elimination, and any changes or disturbances in time pattern, mode of excretion, quality, or quantity of elimination. Also included are any devices used to control excretion.

4 ACTIVITY-EXERCISE PATTERN

Describes pattern of exercise, activity, leisure, and recreation. Includes activities of daily living requiring energy expenditure, such as hygiene, cooking, shopping, eating, working, and home maintenance. Also included are the type, quantity, and quality of exercise, including sports, that describe the typical pattern for the individual. Leisure patterns are also included and describe the activities the client undertakes as recreation either with a group or as an individual. Emphasis is on the activities of high importance or significance and any limitations. Factors that interfere with desired or expected activities for the individual (such as neuromuscular deficits and compensations, dyspnea, angina, or muscle cramping on exertion, and cardiac/pulmonary classification, if appropriate) are also included.

5   SLEEP-REST PATTERN

Describes patterns of sleep, rest, and relaxation. Includes patterns of sleep and rest/relaxation periods during the 24-hour day. Includes perception of the quality and quantity of sleep and rest, perception of energy level after sleep, and any sleep disturbances. Also included are aids to sleep such as medications or nighttime routines that the individual uses.

6   COGNITIVE-PERCEPTUAL PATTERN

Describes sensory-perceptual and cognitive pattern. Includes the adequacy of sensory modes, such as vision, hearing, taste, touch, and smell, and the compensation or prostheses currently used. Reports of pain perception and how pain is managed are included when appropriate. Also included are cognitive functional abilities such as language, memory, judgment, and decision making.

7   SELF-PERCEPTION–SELF-CONCEPT PATTERN

Describes self-concept pattern and perceptions of mood state. Includes the individual's attitudes about self, perception of abilities (cognitive, affective, or physical), body image, identity, general sense of worth, and general emotional pattern. Body posture and movement, eye contact, voice, and speech pattern are included.

8   ROLE-RELATIONSHIP PATTERN

Describes pattern of role engagements and relationships. Includes the individual's perception of the major roles and responsibilities in current life situation. Satisfaction or disturbances in family, work, or social relationships and responsibilities related to these roles are included.

9   SEXUALITY-REPRODUCTIVE PATTERN

Describes patterns of satisfaction or dissatisfaction with sexuality; describes reproductive pattern. Includes the individual's perceived satisfaction or reports of disturbances in his or her sexuality. Included also is the female's reproductive stage (premenopause or postmenopause) and any perceived problems.

10 COPING–STRESS-TOLERANCE PATTERN

Describes general coping pattern and effectiveness of the pattern in terms of stress tolerance. Includes the individual's reserve or capacity to resist challenge to self-integrity, modes of handling stress, family or other support systems, and perceived ability to manage stressful situations.

11 VALUE-BELIEF PATTERN

Describes patterns of values, goals, or beliefs (including spiritual) that guide choices or decisions. Includes what is perceived as important in life, quality of life, and any perceived conflicts in values, beliefs, or expectations that are health related.

BIBLIOGRAPHY

The following references describe functional health patterns, suggested uses of the patterns, and reports of clinical use and research.

Bcyea S, Matzo M. Assessing elders using the functional health pattern assessment model. *Nurse Educ.* 1989;14:32–37.

Bryant SO, Kopeski LM. Psychiatric nursing assessment of the eating disorder client. *Top Clin Nurs.* 1986;8:57–66.

Burns C. Development and content validity testing of a comprehensive classification of diagnoses for pediatric nurse practitioners. *Nurs Diagn.* 1991;2:93–104.

Burns C. *Development and Field Testing of a Classification of Diagnoses for Use by Pediatric Nurse Practitioners* [dissertation]. Eugene, Ore: University of Oregon; 1989.

Coler MS, Vincent KG. Coded nursing diagnoses on axes: a prioritized, computer–ready diagnostic system for psychiatric–mental health nurses. *Arch Psychiatr Nurs.* 1987;1:125–131.

Collard A, Jones DA, Fitzmaurice J. Nursing diagnoses in ambulatory care. In McLane A, ed. *Classification of Nursing Diagnoses: Proceedings of the Seventh Conference.* St Louis, Mo: Mosby; 1987.

Corrigan JO. Functional health pattern assessment in the emergency department. *J Emerg Nurs*. 1986;12:163–167.

Decker SD, Knight L. Functional health pattern assessment: a seasonal farmworker community. *J Comm Health Nurs*. 1990;7:141–151.

de Hulla M. Nursing diagnoses in relation to nausea and vomiting caused by chemotherapy. In Mortensen RA, ed. *Proceedings of the First European Conference on Nursing Diagnoses*. Copenhagen, Denmark: Danish Institute for Health and Nursing Research; 1995.

Di Blasi M, Savage J. Revitalizing a documentation system. *Rehabil Nurs*. 1992;17:27–29.

Dion P, Fitzmaurice J, Baer C. Organization of patient assessment data and nursing diagnosis. In McLane A, ed. *Classification of Nursing Diagnoses: Proceedings of the Seventh Conference*. St Louis, Mo: Mosby; 1987.

Doyer B, Macker N, Radovich M. Functional health patterns: a postanesthesia care unit's approach to identification. *J Post Anesth Nurs*. 1990;5:157–162.

Erdemir F. Utilization of nursing diagnoses by students during a pediatric nursing course in Turkey. *Int J Nurs Terminologies Classifications*. 2003;14:59.

Gilmartin ME. Patient and family education. *Clin Chest Med*. 1986;7:619–627.

Gordon M. Capturing patient problems: Nursing diagnoses and functional health patterns. In *Naming Nursing: Proceedings of the first ACENDIO Ireland/UK Conference in Swansea, Wales, UK*. Bern, Switzerland: Verlag-Hans Huber; 2003.

Gordon M. Nursing diagnosis and nursing theory. *Expert Nurse 8*. Tokyo, Japan: Shorinsha; 2000.

Gordon M, Sato S. Easy to understand functional health patterns. Tokyo, Japan: Shorinsha; 1998.

Gordon M. Classification of nursing diagnoses: functional health patterns and the NANDA taxonomy. In Mortensen RA, ed. *Proceedings of the First European Conference on Nursing Diagnoses*. Copenhagen, Denmark: Danish Institute for Health and Nursing Research; 1995.

Gordon M. *Nursing diagnosis: process and application*. St Louis, Mo: Mosby; 1994.

Gordon M. Practice–based data set for a nursing information system. *J Med Systems*. 1985;9:43–55.

Greenlee KK. Effects of implementation of an operational definition and guidelines for the formulation of nursing diagnoses in a critical care setting. In Carroll-Johnson R, ed. *Classification of Nursing Diagnoses: Proceedings of the Ninth Conference*. St Louis, Mo: Mosby; 1991.

Hanna D, Wyman N. Assessment + diagnosis = care planning: a tool for coordination, *Nurs Manage*. 1989;18:106–109.

Hartman D, Knudson J. Documentation: a nursing data base for initial patient assessment. *Oncol Nurs Forum*. 1991;18:125–130.

Henning M. Comparison of nursing diagnostic statements using a functional health pattern and health history/body systems format. In Carroll-Johnson R, ed. *Classification of Nursing Diagnoses: Proceedings of the Ninth Conference*. St Louis, Mo: Mosby; 1991.

Herberth L, Gosnell DJ. Nursing diagnosis for oncology nursing practice. *Cancer Nurs.* 1987;10:41–51.

Hirschfield-Bartek J, Dow KH. Decreasing documentation time using a patient self-assessment tool. *Oncol Nurs Forum.* 1990;17:251–255.

Hovey JE. Development of a psychiatric nursing assessment tool utilizing functional health patterns. In Rantz MJ, LeMone P, eds. *Classification of Nursing Diagnoses: Proceedings of the Eleventh Conference.* Glendale, Calif: CINAHL Information Systems; 1995.

Johannesma JC. Diagnostic procedures and nursing diagnoses for the elderly. In Mortensen RA, ed. *Proceedings of the First European Conference on Nursing Diagnoses.* Copenhagen, Denmark: Danish Institute for Health and Nursing Research; 1995.

Johnson M, Maas M, Moorhead S. *Nursing outcomes classification* (NIC). St Louis: Mo: Mosby; 2000.

Flanagan J, Jones DA. Patient response to the fast-track experience. *Inter J Terminologies and Classifications.* 2003;14:42.

Jones DA, Foster FB. Further development and testing of a Functional Health Pattern Assessment Screening Tool. In Rantz M, LeMone P, eds. *Classification of Nursing Diagnoses: Proceedings of the Thirteenth Conference.* Glendale, Calif: CINAHL Information Systems; 1999.

Jones DA. Alternative conceptualizations of assessment. In Carroll-Johnson R, Paquette M, eds. *Classification of Nursing Diagnoses: Proceedings of the Tenth Conference.* Philadelphia, Pa: Lippincott; 1994.

Leahy MK. Using nursing diagnosis as an organizing framework in an integrated curriculum. In Jones A, ed. *From Theory to Practice: Abstracts of the Second Nursing Theory Congress.* Toronto, Ontario: University of Toronto Press; 1988.

Levin RF, Crosley JM. Focused data collection for the generation of nursing diagnoses. *J Nurs Staff Dev.* 1906;4:56–64.

McCourt A, ed. *The Specialty Practice of Rehabilitation Nursing: A Core Curriculum.* 3rd ed. Skokie, Ill: Rehabilitation Nursing Foundation; 1993.

McFarland G, Thomas MD. *Psychiatric Mental Health Nursing.* Philadelphia, Pa: Lippincott; 1990.

Monninger E, Padgett D, Fleeger MA. Functional health pattern assessment for BSN students. In Carroll-Johnson R, Paquette M, eds. *Classification of Nursing Diagnoses: Proceedings of the Tenth Conference.* Philadelphia, Pa: Lippincott; 1994.

Monteiro da Cruz, Dina de Almeida Lopes. Nursing diagnosis of patients with Chagas disease. In Rantz M, LeMone P, eds. *Classification of Nursing Diagnoses: Proceedings of the Eleventh Conference.* Glendale, Calif: CINAHL Information Systems; 1995.

Mumma CM, ed. *Rehabilitation Nursing: Concepts and Practice: A Core Curriculum.* 2nd ed. Skokie, Ill: Rehabilitation Nursing Foundation; 1987.

Nettle C, Jones N, Pifer P. Community nursing diagnoses. *Comm Health Nurs.* 1989;6:135–145.

FUNCTIONAL HEALTH PATTERNS TYPOLOGY

NANDA International. NANDA nursing diagnosis classification, taxonomy II. In *NANDA International Nursing Diagnoses: Definitions and Classification, 2005–2006*. Philadelphia, PA: NANDA International; 2005. (Taxonomy domains adapted from Gordon M, *Functional Health Patterns Framework*.)

O'Connell BO. Does an assessment format influence diagnostic outcomes? A comparison between Gordon's Functional Health Patterns and a review of biological systems assessment formats. In Mortensen RA, ed. *Proceedings of the First European Conference on Nursing Diagnoses*. Copenhagen, Denmark: Danish Institute for Health and Nursing Research; 1995.

Oud NE. Nursing diagnoses and applications in psychiatric and mental nursing. In Mortensen RA, ed. *Proceedings of the First European Conference on Nursing Diagnoses*. Copenhagen, Denmark: Danish Institute for Health and Nursing Research; 1995.

Phelan C, Finnell MD, Mottla KA. A patient self-assessment tool for cardiac rehabilitation. *Rehabil Nurs*. 1989;14:81, 84–87.

Rantz M, Miller TV. How diagnoses are changing in long-term care. *Am J Nurs*. 1987;87:360–361.

Rossi L. Organizing data for nursing diagnosis using functional health patterns. In McLane A, ed. *Classification of Nursing Diagnoses: Proceedings of the Seventh Conference*. St Louis, Mo: Mosby; 1987.

Tompkins ES. In support of the discipline of nursing: a nursing assessment. *Nurs Connect*. 1989;2:21–29.

Volpato MP. Nursing diagnoses in medical-surgical patients. *Inter J Nurs Terminologies and Classifications*. 2003;14:57.

Ward CR. Proportion of specific agreement as a measure of intrarater reliability in the diagnostic process. In McLane A, ed. *Classification of Nursing Diagnoses: Proceedings of the Seventh Conference*. St Louis, Mo: Mosby; 1987.

Westwell J et al. Health patterns assessment: a form designed to allow psychiatric nurses to practice theoretical pluralism. In Jones A, ed. *From Theory to Practice: Abstracts of the Second Nursing Theory Congress*. Toronto, Ontario: University of Toronto Press; 1988.

Woodtli MA, Van Ort S. Nursing diagnoses and functional health patterns in patients receiving external radiation therapy: cancer of the head and neck. *Nurs Diagn*. 1991;2:171–180.

Functional Health Patterns Assessment Guidelines

FUNCTIONAL HEALTH PATTERNS ASSESSMENT GUIDELINES

This section contains assessment guidelines based on the health pattern definitions. Functional health patterns provide a format for the admission assessment and a database for nursing diagnoses. There are two phases in assessment: history taking and examination. A nursing history provides a description of a client's functional patterns. The description is from the individual's (or parent/guardian's), family's, or community representative's perspective and provides data in the form of verbal reports. These reports are elicited by questions that assist clients to tell the history and current status of their health and health management. Observations in the examination phase provide data on pattern indicators and verification of information obtained during history taking.

The formats for assessment that follow are designed to elicit information in a systematic manner. They are screening formats for the collection of a basic nursing database in any specialty, for any age group, and at any point in the wellness-illness continuum. Questions and examination items tap into areas of all current nursing diagnoses. If data indicate that a problem or potential problem (dysfunctional pattern) may be present, diagnostic hypotheses (nursing diagnoses) should be generated to direct further information collection. This directs the search for the diagnostic or critical characteristics of each possibility.

Nurses practicing in a specialty area may desire in-depth assessments of certain patterns. Both the history (subjective data) and the examination (objective data) can be expanded relative to disease, disability, age, and other client-specific factors. For example, a client's activity-exercise pattern requires an in-depth assessment when the client has a disease that affects this pattern.

Diagnoses are grouped under the same pattern areas as they are in the assessment guidelines and can be used to label data in a pattern area. As discussed previously, this facilitates the process of moving from assessment data to diagnosis.

ADULT ASSESSMENT

Nursing History

1. **HEALTH-PERCEPTION–HEALTH-MANAGEMENT PATTERN**

    a. How has general health been?

    b. Any colds in the past year? If appropriate: Absences from work/school?

    c. Most important things done to keep healthy? Think these things make a difference to health? (include family folk remedies, if appropriate). Breast self-examination? Use cigarettes? Drugs? Ever had a drinking problem? When was your last drink?

    d. Accidents (home, work, driving)? Falls?

    e. In past, easy to find ways to follow suggestions of doctors or nurses?

    f. If appropriate: What do you think caused this illness? Action taken when symptoms perceived? Results of action?

    g. If appropriate: What is important to you while you are here? How can we be most helpful?

2. **NUTRITIONAL-METABOLIC PATTERN**

    a. Typical daily food intake? (describe) Supplements?

    b. Typical daily fluid intake? (describe)

    c. Weight loss/gain? (amount) Height loss/gain? (amount)

    d. Appetite?

    e. Food or eating: Discomfort? Swallowing? Diet restrictions? If appropriate: Breastfeeding? Problems with breastfeeding?

    f. Heal well or poorly?

    g. Skin problems: Lesions, dryness?

    h. Dental problems?

11

3. ELIMINATION PATTERN

a. Bowel elimination pattern? (describe) Frequency? Character? Discomfort? Problem in control? Laxatives?
b. Urinary elimination pattern? (describe) Frequency? Discomfort? Problem in control?
c. Excess perspiration? Odor problems?

4. ACTIVITY-EXERCISE PATTERN

a. Sufficient energy for desired/required activities?
b. Exercise pattern? Type? Regularity?
c. Spare time (leisure) activities? Child: Play activities?
d. Perceived ability for: (code for level according to Functional Levels Code key below)

Feeding _____	Grooming _____
Bathing _____	General mobility _____
Toileting _____	Cooking _____
Bed mobility _____	Home maintenance _____
Dressing _____	Shopping _____

Functional Levels Code

Level 0:	Full self care
Level I:	Requires use of equipment or device
Level II:	Requires assistance or supervision of another person
Level III:	Requires assistance or supervision of another person and equipment or device
Level IV:	Is dependent and does not participate

5. SLEEP-REST PATTERN

a. Generally rested and ready for daily activities after sleep?
b. Sleep-onset problems? Aids? Dreams (nightmares)? Early awakening?
c. Rest/relaxation periods?

6. COGNITIVE-PERCEPTUAL PATTERN

   a. Hearing difficulty? Aid?
   b. Vision? Wear glasses? Last checked?
   c. Any change in memory lately?
   d. Easy/difficult to make decisions?
   e. Easiest way for you to learn things? Any difficulty learning?
   f. Any discomfort? Pain? How do you manage it?

7. SELF-PERCEPTION–SELF-CONCEPT PATTERN

   a. How would you describe yourself? Most of the time, feel good (not so good) about yourself?
   b. Changes in your body or the things you can do? Are these problematic for you?
   c. Changes in way you feel about yourself or your body (since illness started)?
   d. Find things frequently make you angry? Annoyed? Fearful? Anxious? Depressed? What helps?
   e. Ever feel you lose hope? Not able to control things in life? What helps?

8. ROLE-RELATIONSHIP PATTERN

   a. Live alone? Family? Family structure? (draw diagram)
   b. Any family problems you have difficulty handling? (nuclear/extended)
   c. How does family usually handle problems?
   d. Family depend on you for things? How are you managing?
   e. If appropriate: How do family/others feel about your illness/hospitalization?
   f. If appropriate: Problems with children? Difficulty handling?
   g. Belong to social groups? Close friends? Feel lonely? (frequency)

    h. Things generally go well for you at work? (school?) If appropriate: Income sufficient for needs?

    i. Feel part of (or isolated in) neighborhood where living?

9. SEXUALITY-REPRODUCTIVE PATTERN

    a. If appropriate to age/situation: Sexual relationships satisfying? Changes? Problems?

    b. If appropriate: Use of contraceptives? Problems?

    c. Female: When menstruation started? Last menstrual period? Menstrual problems? Para? Gravida?

10. COPING–STRESS-TOLERANCE PATTERN

    a. Any big changes in your life in the last year or two? Crisis?

    b. Who's most helpful in talking things over? Available to you now?

    c. Tense a lot of the time? What helps? Use any medicines, drugs, alcohol?

    d. When (if) big problems (or any problems) occur in your life, how do you handle them?

    e. Most of the time, is this way(s) successful?

11. VALUE-BELIEF PATTERN

    a. Generally get things you want out of life? Important plans for the future?

    b. Religion important in your life? If appropriate: Does this help when difficulties arise?

    c. If appropriate: Will being here interfere with any religious practices?

12. OTHER

    a. Any other things that we have not talked about that you would like to mention?

    b. Questions?

FUNCTIONAL HEALTH PATTERNS ASSESSMENT GUIDELINES

SCREENING EXAMINATION FORMAT

(Add other pattern indicators to expand the examination as appropriate)

    a. General appearance, grooming, hygiene _____

    b. Oral mucous membranes
       (color, moistness, lesions) _____

    c. Teeth: Dentures _____ Cavities _____ Missing _____

    d. Hears whisper? _____

    e. Reads newsprint? _____ Glasses? _____

    f. Pulse (rate) _____ (rhythm) _____ (strength) _____

    g. Respiration _____ (depth) _____ (rhythm) _____

    h. Breath sounds _____ Blood pressure _____

    i. Hand grip _____ Can pick up pencil? _____

    j. Range of motion (joints) _____
       Muscle firmness (tone) _____

    k. Skin: Bony prominences _____ Lesions _____
       Color changes _____

    l. Gait _____ Posture _____ Absent body part _____

    m. *Demonstrated ability for: (code for level)*

Feeding _____	Grooming _____
Bathing _____	General mobility _____
Toileting _____	Cooking _____
Bed mobility _____	Home maintenance _____
Dressing _____	Shopping _____

    n. Intravenous, drainage, suction, etc. (specify) _____

    o. Actual weight _____ Reported weight _____

    p. Height _____ Temperature _____

During history and examination:

    q. Orientation _____ Grasp ideas and questions
       (abstract, concrete)? _____

    r. Language spoken _____
       Voice and speech pattern _____

    s. Vocabulary level _____

    t. Eye contact _____ Attention span (distraction) _____

    u. Nervous (5) or relaxed (1) (rate from 1 to 5) _____

    v. Assertive (5) or passive (1) (rate from 1 to 5) _____

    w. Interaction with family member, guardian, other
        (if present) _____

INFANT AND YOUNG CHILD ASSESSMENT

When a new infant or child is added to a nurse's caseload, a comprehensive assessment is done to establish a database for developmental assessment and for nursing diagnosis and treatment. Information is needed on (1) the development of each functional pattern and anatomical growth, (2) current health patterns, and (3) family health and the home environment in which the infant or child is developing. Minimally, the admission nursing history and examination has to screen for high-incidence problems. The questions and items listed below can be used as a guide for a comprehensive parent-child health history or used selectively for problem screening.

NURSING HISTORY

1. HEALTH-PERCEPTION–HEALTH-MANAGEMENT PATTERN

Parent's report of:

    a. Mother's pregnancy/labor/delivery history (of this infant, of others)?

    b. Infant's health status since birth?

    c. Adherence to routine health checks for the infant/child? Immunizations?

    d. Infections in the infant/child? Child's absences from school?

    e. If appropriate: Infant's/child's medical problem, treatment, and prognosis?

    f. If appropriate: Actions taken by parents when signs and/or symptoms were perceived?

    g. If appropriate: Has it been easy to follow doctor's or nurse's suggestions?

    h. Preventive health practices (e.g., diaper change, utensils, and clothes)?
    i. Do parents smoke? Around children?
    j. Accidents? Frequency?
    k. Infant's crib toys (safety)? Carrying safety? Car safety?
    l. Parents' safety practices (e.g., household products and medicines)?

Parents (self):
    a. Parents'/family's general health status?

2. NUTRITIONAL-METABOLIC PATTERN

Parent's report of the infant's/child's:
    a. Breast/bottle feeding? Intake (estimated)? Sucking strength?
    b. Appetite? Feeding discomfort?
    c. 24-hour intake of nutrients? Supplements?
    d. Eating behavior? Food preferences? Conflicts over food?
    e. Birth weight? Current weight?
    f. Skin problems: Rashes, lesions, others?

Parents (self):
    a. Parents'/family's nutritional status? Problems?

3. ELIMINATION PATTERN

Parent's report of the infant's/child's:
    a. Bowel elimination pattern? (describe) Frequency? Character? Discomfort?
    b. Diaper changes? (describe routine)
    c. Urinary elimination pattern? (describe) Number of wet diapers per day? (estimate amount) Stream (strong, dribble)?
    d. Excess perspiration? Odor?

Parents (self):
    a. Elimination pattern? Problems?

4. ACTIVITY-EXERCISE PATTERN

Parent's report of:
   a. Bathing routine (when, how, where, and what type of soap)?
   b. Dressing routine (clothing worn, changes inside/outside home)?
   c. Typical day's activity for the infant/child? (e.g., hours spent in crib, being carried, playing; type of toys used)
   d. Infant's/child's general activity level? Tolerance?
   e. Perception of infant's/child's strength (strong or fragile)?
   f. Child's self care ability (bathing, feeding, toileting, dressing, grooming)?

Parents (self):
   a. Activity/exercise/leisure pattern? Child care? Home maintenance?

5. SLEEP-REST PATTERN

Parent's report of:
   a. Sleep pattern of the infant/child: Estimated hours?
   b. Infant's/child's restlessness? Nightmares? Nocturia?
   c. Infant's sleep position? Body movements?

Parents (self):
   a. Sleep pattern?

6. COGNITIVE-PERCEPTUAL PATTERN

Parent's report of:
   a. General responsiveness of the infant/child?
   b. Infant's response to talking? Noise? Objects? Touch?
   c. Infant's following of objects with eyes? Response to crib toys?
   d. Learning (changes noted)? What is being taught to the infant/child?

    e. Noises/vocalizations? Speech pattern? Words? Sentences?

    f. Use of stimulation: Talking, games, what else?

    g. Vision, hearing, touch, kinesthesia of the infant/child?

    h. Child's ability to tell name, time, address, telephone number?

    i. Infant's/child's ability to identify needs (hunger, thirst, pain, discomfort)?

Parents (self):

    a. Problems with vision, hearing, touch, other senses?

    b. Difficulties making decisions? Judgments?

7. SELF-PERCEPTION–SELF-CONCEPT PATTERN

Parent's report of:

    a. Infant's/child's mood state (irritability)?

    b. Child's sense of worth, identity, competency?

Child's report of:

    a. Mood state?

    b. Many/few friends? Liked by others?

    c. Self-perception (good most of time? hard to be good?)

    d. Ever lonely?

    e. Fears (transient/frequent)?

Parents (self):

    a. General sense of worth, identity, competency?

    b. Self-perception as parents?

8. ROLE-RELATIONSHIP PATTERN

Parent's report of:

    a. Family/household structure?

    b. Family problems/stressors?

    c. Interactions among family members and infant (or child)?

    d. Infant's/child's response to separation?

    e. Child: Dependency?

    f. Child: Play pattern?

    g. Child: Temper tantrums? Discipline problems? School adjustment?

Parents (self):

    a. Role engagements? Satisfaction?

    b. Work, social, marital relationships?

9. SEXUALITY-REPRODUCTIVE PATTERN

Parent's report of child's:

    a. Feeling of maleness/femaleness?

    b. Questions regarding sexuality? How parent responds?

Parents (self):

    a. If applicable: Reproductive history?

    b. Sexual satisfaction/problems?

10. COPING–STRESS-TOLERANCE PATTERN

Parent's report of:

    a. What produces stress in child? Level of stress tolerance?

    b. Child's pattern of handling problems, frustrations, anger?

Parents (self):

    a. Life stressors? Family stress?

    b. Strategies for handling problems? Support systems?

11. VALUE-BELIEF PATTERN

Parent's report of:

    a. Child's moral development, choice behavior, commitments?

Parents (self):

    a. Things important in life (values, spirituality)? Desires for the future?

    b. If appropriate: Perceived impact of disease on goals?

12. OTHER

   a. Any other things that we haven't talked about that
      you'd like to mention? Any questions?

SCREENING EXAMINATION FORMAT

   a. General appearance of infant/child _____
   b. General appearance of parents _____
   c. Child's height/weight _____
      Structural growth and development _____
   d. Skin color, hydration, rashes, lesions _____
   e. If warranted examine: Child's/infant's urine and
      stool _____
   f. Reflexes (appropriate to age?) _____
      Blood pressure _____
   g. Breathing pattern: Rate, rhythm _____
   h. Heart sounds: Rate, rhythm _____
   i. Infant/child: Responsiveness, cognitive-perceptual
      development _____
   j. Child: Eye contact, speech pattern,
      posturing _____
   k. Smiling response (infant) _____
   l. Social interaction (child):
      Aggressive/withdrawn? _____
   m. Response to vocalizations? Requests? _____

FAMILY ASSESSMENT

The 11 functional health pattern areas are also applicable to
the assessment of families. Families are the primary client in
community health nursing. In some cases a family assessment may be indicated (1) in the care of an infant or child
whose development is influenced by family health patterns
or (2) when an adult has certain health problems that (a)
can be influenced by family patterns or (b) can influence
these patterns. The following guidelines provide information
on family functioning.

1. HEALTH-PERCEPTION–HEALTH-MANAGEMENT PATTERN

History:

    a. How has family's general health been (in last few years)?

    b. Colds in past year? Absence from work/school?

    c. Most important things to keep healthy? Think these make a difference to health? (include family folk remedies, if appropriate.)

    d. Family members' use of cigarettes, alcohol, drugs?

    e. Immunizations? Health care provider? Frequency of checkups?

    f. Accidents (home, work, school, driving) (if appropriate: Storage of drugs, cleaning products, use of scatter rugs, etc.)?

    g. In past, easy to find ways to follow suggestions of doctors, nurses, social workers (if appropriate)?

    h. Things important to family's health that I could help with?

Examination:

    a. General appearance of family members and home.

    b. If appropriate: Storage of medicines, location of cribs, playpens, stove, scatter rugs, hazards, other potentially harmful objects.

2. NUTRITIONAL-METABOLIC PATTERN

History:

    a. Typical family meal pattern/food intake? (describe) Supplements (e.g., vitamins, types of snacks)?

    b. Typical family fluid intake? (describe) Supplements: type (e.g., fruit juices, soft drinks, coffee)?

    c. Appetite? Problems? Dental care (frequency)?

    d. Anyone have skin problems? Healing problems?

Examination:
    a. If opportunity available: Refrigerator contents, meal preparation, contents of meal, etc.

3. ELIMINATION PATTERN

History:
    a. Family use of laxatives, other aids?
    b. Problems in waste/garbage disposal?
    c. Pet animals' waste disposal (indoor/outdoor)?
    d. If indicated: Problems with flies, roaches, rodents?
Examination:
    a. If opportunity available: Examine toilet facilities, garbage disposal, pet waste disposal; indicators of risk for flies, roaches, rodents.

4. ACTIVITY-EXERCISE PATTERN

History:
    a. In general, does family get a lot of exercise or little exercise? Type? Regularity?
    b. Family leisure activities? Active or passive?
    c. Problems in shopping (transportation), cooking, keeping up the house, budgeting for food, clothes, housekeeping, housing costs?
Examination:
    a. Pattern of general home maintenance, personal maintenance.

5. SLEEP-REST PATTERN

History:
    a. Generally, do family members seem to be well rested and ready for school or work?
    b. Sufficient sleeping space and quiet?
    c. Does family find time to relax?
Examination:
    a. If opportunity available: Observe sleeping space and arrangements.

6. COGNITIVE-PERCEPTUAL PATTERN

History:
   a. Visual or hearing problems? How managed?
   b. Any big decisions family has had to make? How made?

Examination:
   a. If indicated: Language spoken at home
   b. Grasp of ideas and questions (abstract or concrete)
   c. Vocabulary level

7. SELF-PERCEPTION–SELF-CONCEPT PATTERN

History:
   a. Most of time family feels good (not so good) about themselves as a family?
   b. General mood of family? Happy? Anxious? Depressed? What helps family mood?

Examination:
   a. General mood state: relaxed (1) or nervous (5); rate from 1 to 5 _____
   b. Members generally passive (1) or assertive (5); rate from 1 to 5 _____

8. ROLE-RELATIONSHIP PATTERN

History:
   a. Family (or household) members' age and family structure? (draw diagram)
   b. Any family problems that are difficult to handle (nuclear/extended)? Child rearing? If appropriate: Spouse ever get rough with you? Children?
   c. Relationships good (not so good) among family members? Siblings?
   d. If appropriate: Income sufficient for needs?
   e. Feel part of (or isolated from) community? Neighbors?

24

Examination:
   a. Interaction among family members (if present)
   b. Observed family leadership roles

9. SEXUALITY-REPRODUCTIVE PATTERN

History:
   a. If appropriate (sexual partner within household or situation): Sexual relations satisfying? Changes? Problems?
   b. Use of family planning? Contraceptives? Problems?
   c. If appropriate (to age of children): Feel comfortable in explaining/discussing sexual subjects?

Examination:
   None

10. COPING-STRESS-TOLERANCE PATTERN

History:
   a. Any big changes within family in last few years?
   b. Family tense or relaxed most of time? When tense, what helps? Anyone use medicines, drugs, alcohol to decrease tension? Support each other?
   c. When family problems arise, how handled?
   d. Most of the time is this way(s) successful?

Examination:
   None

11. VALUE-BELIEF PATTERN

History:
   a. Generally, family get things they want out of life?
   b. Important things for the future?
   c. Any "rules" in the family that everyone believes are important?
   d. Religion important in family? Does this help when difficulties arise?

Examination:
   None

COMMUNITY ASSESSMENT*

Communities develop health patterns. In some practice settings the community is the primary client. In other cases an individual client or a family may have, or be predisposed to, certain problems that require an assessment of certain community patterns. The following are guidelines for a comprehensive community assessment, but particular community patterns may be relevant to care of an individual or family. In addition, if a community health nurse or agency does not wish to obtain an in-depth study of a community, screening of functional patterns is possible by selecting items from the examination sections.

1. HEALTH-PERCEPTION–HEALTH-MANAGEMENT PATTERN

History (community representatives):

a. In general, what is the health/wellness level of the population on a scale of 1 to 5, with 5 being high? Any major health problems?

b. Any strong cultural patterns influencing health practices?

c. Do people feel they have access to health services?

d. Is there demand for any particular health services or prevention programs?

e. Do people feel fire, police, safety programs are sufficient?

Examination (community records):

a. Morbidity, mortality, disability rates (by age group, if appropriate).

---

*Community assessment items are adapted from Gikow F, Kucharski P. Functional health pattern assessment of a community. Paper presented at: American Public Health Association, 112th annual meeting; November 13, 1984; Anaheim, Calif. Gikow and Kucharski used the functional assessment to evaluate health-related needs of a community served by their agency.

    b. Accident rates (by district, if appropriate)
    c. Currently operating health facilities (types)
    d. Ongoing health promotion/prevention programs, utilization rates
    e. Ratios of health professionals to population
    f. Laws regarding drinking age
    g. Arrest statistics for drug use and/or drunk driving by age group

2. NUTRITIONAL-METABOLIC PATTERN

History (community representatives):

    a. In general, do most people seem well nourished? Children? Elderly?
    b. Food supplement programs? Food stamps: Rate of use?
    c. Is cost of foods reasonable in this area relative to income?
    d. Are stores accessible for most? Meals on Wheels available?
    e. Water supply and quality? Testing services (if most have own wells)? If appropriate: Water usage cost? Any drought restrictions?
    f. Any concern that community growth will exceed good water supply?
    g. Are heating/cooling costs manageable for most? Programs?

Examination:

    a. General appearance (nutrition, teeth, clothing appropriate for climate). Children? Adults? Elderly?
    b. Food purchases (observations at food store checkout counters).
    c. "Junk" food (e.g., machines in schools).

27

3. ELIMINATION PATTERN

History (community representatives):

    a. Major kinds of wastes (e.g., industrial, sewage)? Disposal systems? Recycling programs? Any problems perceived by community?

    b. Pest control? Food service inspection (e.g., restaurants, street vendors)?

Examination (community records):

    a. Communicable disease statistics

    b. Air pollution statistics

4. ACTIVITY-EXERCISE PATTERN

History (community representatives):

    a. How do people find the transportation here? To work? For recreation? To health care?

    b. Do people (seniors, others) have/use community centers? Recreation facilities for children? Adults? Seniors?

    c. Is housing adequate (availability, cost)? Public housing?

Examination:

    a. Recreation/cultural programs

    b. Assistance for the disabled

    c. Residential centers, nursing homes, rehabilitation facilities relative to population needs

    d. External maintenance of homes, yards, apartment houses

    e. General activity level (e.g., bustling, quiet)

5. SLEEP-REST PATTERN

History (community representatives):

    a. Generally quiet at night in most neighborhoods?

    b. Usual business hours? Are industries active around the clock?

Examination:
   a. Activity/noise levels in business district, residential area

6. COGNITIVE-PERCEPTUAL PATTERN

History:
   a. Do most groups speak English? Bilingual?
   b. Educational level of population?
   c. Schools seen as good or need improving? Adult education desired or available?
   d. Types of problems that require community decisions? Decision-making process? What is best way to get things done/changed in community?

Examination:
   a. School facilities, dropout rate
   b. Community government structure, decision-making lines

7. SELF-PERCEPTION–SELF-CONCEPT PATTERN

History (community representatives):
   a. Good community to live in? Status going up, down, or staying about the same?
   b. Old community? Fairly new?
   c. Does any age group predominate?
   d. People's mood, in general: Enjoying life? Stressed? Feeling "down"?
   e. People generally have the kinds of abilities needed in this community?
   f. Community/neighborhood functions? Parades?

Examination:
   a. Racial, ethnic mix (if appropriate)
   b. Socioeconomic level
   c. General observations of mood

8. ROLE-RELATIONSHIP PATTERN

History (community representatives):

   a. Do people seem to get along well together here? Places where people tend to go to socialize?
   b. Do people feel they are heard by the government? High or low participation in meetings?
   c. Enough work/jobs for everybody? Are wages good/fair? Do people seem to like the type of work available (happy in their jobs or feel job stress)?
   d. Any problems with riots, violence in the neighborhoods? Family violence? Problems with child/spouse/elder abuse?
   e. Does community get along with adjacent communities? Do people collaborate on any community projects?
   f. Do neighbors seem to support each other?
   g. Community get-togethers?

Examination:

   a. Observation of interactions (generally or at specific meetings)
   b. Statistics on interpersonal violence
   c. Statistics on employment, income, poverty
   d. Divorce rate

9. SEXUALITY-REPRODUCTIVE PATTERN

History (community representatives):

   a. Average family size?
   b. Do people feel there are any problems with pornography, prostitution, other?
   c. Do people want/support sex education in schools/community?

Examination:

   a. Family sizes and types of households
   b. Male/female ratio

30

   c. Average maternal age, maternal mortality rate, infant mortality rate

   d. Teen pregnancy rate

   e. Abortion rate

   f. Sexual violence statistics

   g. Laws/regulations regarding information on birth control

10. COPING–STRESS-TOLERANCE PATTERN

History (community representatives):

   a. Any groups that seem to be under stress?

   b. Need/availability of phone help lines? Support groups (health related, other)?

Examination:

   a. Statistics on delinquency, drug abuse, alcoholism, suicide, psychiatric illness

   b. Unemployment rate by race, ethnic group, sex

11. VALUE-BELIEF PATTERN

History (community representatives):

   a. Community values: What seem to be the top four things that people living here see as important in their lives? (note health-related values, priorities)

   b. Do people tend to get involved in causes/local fund-raising campaigns? (note if any are health related)

   c. Are there religious groups in the community? Churches available?

   d. Do people tend to tolerate or not tolerate differences or socially deviant behavior?

Examination:

   a. Zoning/conservation laws

   b. Scan of community government health committee reports (goals, priorities)

   c. Health budget relative to total budget

CRITICAL CARE ASSESSMENT

Clients who are critically ill, such as those with severe respiratory, cardiac, neurological, or psychological instability, are unable to respond to a full functional health pattern assessment. At times, examination and observation are the major data collection methods used during the critical phase of an illness. The client may not have the energy, capacity, or attention span to provide a health history. Nurses caring for critically ill individuals need to use screening techniques and be sensitive to cues of high-incidence diagnoses. Assessment of particular organ systems and other observational data would be added to the following items that screen for high-frequency/high-treatment-priority nursing diagnoses.

1. **HEALTH-PERCEPTION–HEALTH-MANAGEMENT PATTERN**
   a. Risk for infection (Break in skin from trauma or surgical incision, immunosuppression, debilitation, chronic disease, stasis of body fluids)? Specify area of risk (e.g., general or skin, respiratory, urinary)
   b. Risk for injury (impaired judgment, reduced level of consciousness, sensory-motor impairment, hearing and visual acuity, syncope, ability to use call light)?
   c. Understanding of health status (explanations needed)?

2. **NUTRITIONAL-METABOLIC PATTERN**
   a. Risk for nutritional deficit (intake/parenteral fluids, protein, vitamins, minerals)?
   b. Risk for pressure ulcer (bed mobility, skin over bony prominences, presence of restraints or casts, shear, friction, presence of traction)?
   c. Risk for ineffective thermoregulation (prematurity, head injury, hypothermia, hyperthermia)?

    d. Risk for fluid volume deficit (hypermetabolic states, intake-output)?

    e. Risk for aspiration (depressed cough and gag reflexes, level of consciousness, swallowing, gastric residual, tracheostomy, endotracheal tube)?

3. ELIMINATION PATTERN

    a. Risk for constipation/impaction (last bowel movement)?

    b. Risk for diarrhea, bowel incontinence?

    c. Urinary incontinence (catheter)?

4. ACTIVITY-EXERCISE PATTERN

    a. Risk for activity intolerance (respiratory, cardiac, circulatory problems; shortness of breath; dyspnea at rest or in-bed activities)?

    b. Risk for ineffective airway clearance (on frequent suctioning; rhonchi, wheezes, moist rales, crackles; decreased breath sounds; respiratory problems)?

    c. Ineffective breathing pattern (blood gases, respiratory rate and depth, compensatory position changes)?

    d. Risk for joint contractures (immobilization—bed rest prolonged more than 24 hours, impaired bed mobility)?

    e. Self care deficit (level 1-4, total, or specify: bathing-hygiene, toileting, feeding, dressing-grooming)?

    f. Risk for disuse syndrome (immobilization, paralysis, level of consciousness, 24-hour bed rest)?

5. SLEEP-REST PATTERN

    a. Risk for sleep-pattern disturbance (concerns, fears, noise, interruptions, sleep-onset delay)?

6. COGNITIVE-PERCEPTUAL PATTERN

a. Sensory deficits (hearing, vision)?

b. Client/family decisional conflict (need for decisions, client's decision-making competency, treatment preferences documented)?

c. Impaired thought processes (confusion: general or nocturnal; hallucinations)?

d. Sensory deprivation or overload (monitors, isolation)?

e. Pain (report of severe discomfort/pain, guarding behavior, muscle tension, heart rate increases)?

f. Knowledge sufficient to reduce fear/anxiety (understanding of situation, treatments, care)?

7. SELF-PERCEPTION–SELF-CONCEPT PATTERN

a. Fear/anxiety (client verbal report, focus, family or other verbal report, focus of fear)?

b. Powerlessness (reported feelings of control or lack of control)?

c. Hope (expresses hope or hopelessness)?

d. Self-esteem/worth disturbance (expressions of guilt, perception of ability to deal with crisis)?

8. ROLE-RELATIONSHIP PATTERN

a. Communication (verbal/nonverbal system, language)?

b. Family processes/coping (when appropriate) (interactions, role adjustment, need for information, understanding of family role in ICU)?

c. Grieving (when appropriate: perception of loss)?

d. Role performance (emergency situations, e.g., child care responsibilities)?

e. Parental role conflict (parental role confusion, family role conflicts)?

9. SEXUALITY-REPRODUCTIVE PATTERN

a. Usually deferred unless pertains to the client's condition

10. COPING–STRESS-TOLERANCE PATTERN

a. Coping (anxiety level of client, family; compromised, disabling)?

11. VALUE-BELIEF PATTERN

a. Spiritual distress (questions meanings, e.g., of suffering; inner conflict about beliefs; anger, nightmares, sleep disturbance)?

Use of Diagnostic Categories in Clinical Practice

Nursing diagnoses, in conjunction with medical diagnoses, provide a focus for most nursing care activities. Because issues of cost containment, case management, reimbursement, and quality assessment and assurance play such a large part in professional practice models, the following clinical applications of the diagnostic categories in this manual are suggested.

DIAGNOSIS AND TREATMENT WITHIN THE NURSING PROCESS

a. The nursing process is a problem-identification and problem-solving process. The process is initiated with assessment (as the information collected provides cues to the health of an individual, family, or community).

   Some cues are diagnostic. A diagnostic cue is a critical defining characteristic, or clinical indicator, of a functional, dysfunctional, or potentially dysfunctional health state. Consider a diagnostic cue important until investigation of its meaning proves otherwise. Use diagnostic categories as possible explanations of the meaning of cues. Consider alternative possible meanings for a cue or cue cluster (e.g., anxiety, fear, depression).

b. Investigate the most likely possibilities first. Assess the presence or absence of diagnostic cues. These cues are the criteria that must be present before the diagnostic label is used; they are few in number.

c. Investigate the probable causes of the problem. Determine the etiological and/or related factors that, if altered, would have the greatest positive effect. Focus intervention on these factors first (e.g., self care deficit, level III, related to activity intolerance). Avoid premature closure; be sure diagnostic cues are present to justify the diagnostic statement (problem *and* etiology).

e. Syndromes do not have etiological or related factors specified. The probable cause is built into the diagnostic label (e.g., see post-traumatic, rape, translocation, disuse, sudden infant death).

f.   High-risk diagnoses have risk factors. Intervene on the risk factors that can have the greatest impact in preventing the condition. Focus intervention on these factors first. Risk diagnoses do not have etiological/related factors.

The key role of nursing diagnosis in nursing process may be seen in the diagram on pp. 40–41; it depicts the components of the nursing process.

DOCUMENTATION

Use diagnostic category labels to describe the problem or potential problem. Use the client reports and observations to describe subjective and objective data (if problem-oriented format is used). Etiological or related factors document the probable cause(s) that focuses nursing care planning. (Conditions currently not on accepted diagnostic listings should be documented in descriptive terms and subjected to clinical study.) Diagnoses, diagnosis-specific interventions, and diagnosis specific outcomes are sufficiently developed for incorporating into computerized systems.

COMMUNICATION

Use diagnostic category labels as a concise summary of the client's condition in shift and administrative reports, discharge planning, referrals, and case conferences.

CONSULTATIONS

Use cues and/or diagnostic category labels as a concise summary when requesting clinical nurse–specialist consultation. Diagnostic category labels are also useful when requesting consultation and specialized services to treat nursing diagnoses (e.g., nutritional, physical, occupational, recreational, art/music therapy). The consultant's report is also written using nursing diagnostic terms.

COMPONENTS OF NURSING PROCESS

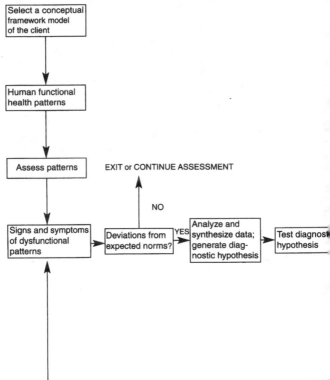

USE OF DIAGNOSTIC CATEGORIES IN CLINICAL PRACTICE

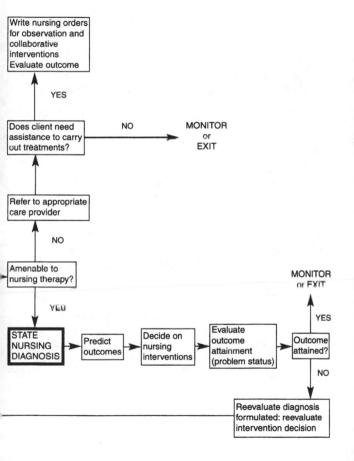

QUALITY, STANDARDS OF CARE, AND NATIONAL GUIDELINES

Use diagnostic categories and their components as topics for process and outcome audits in a quality-improvement program. Assess the use of diagnoses and the accuracy of diagnostic judgments (process audit). Establish treatment guidelines for diagnoses, that is, intervention and outcome standards and criteria for their measurement. Implement national guidelines focusing on nursing diagnoses (pain, decubitus ulcer, depression, etc.) and developed by the United States Agency for Healthcare Research and Quality (AHRQ). See their Web site.

COST OF NURSING CARE, REIMBURSEMENT, AND STAFFING

Diagnostic categories can be used as the focus of client classification. This is necessary for costing out nursing care, reimbursement, and staffing decisions. In determining cost of services, it is necessary to obtain a refined measure of resources consumed, such as that provided by nursing diagnoses. Determining cost of treatment based on nursing diagnosis, medical diagnosis, and an acuity factor is currently in the experimental stage.

CASE MANAGEMENT

Diagnostic category labels are used in conjunction with medical diagnoses to focus case management. Nursing diagnosis–specific outcomes and medical diagnosis–specific outcomes are used in outcome-focused case management.

CRITICAL PATHS

Nursing diagnostic categories and client strengths (identified during functional assessment) (1) describe variances that influence the path to a projected outcome for a disease or (2) are the basis for the construction of a nursing diagnosis critical path (with other nursing and medical diagnoses as variances). Critical paths are a way of scheduling recovery (attainment of outcomes) within a time and process (intervention/evaluation) framework.

RESEARCH AND THEORY DEVELOPMENT

Diagnostic categories and their components provide concise summaries of the underlying concepts. They are the focus of clinical nursing research and are used in midrange theory building within nursing science. Research on the effectiveness of interventions for nursing diagnoses are ongoing.

Documentation:
Format and Example

DOCUMENTATION: FORMAT AND EXAMPLE

Following an admission assessment, nursing diagnoses and treatment plans are documented in the client's record. Documentation is critically important for legal purposes, continuity of care, costing-out nursing services, reimbursement, and planning staffing of units. Currently there is a transition from paper charts and a Kardex to computerized documentation in an electronic information system.

A commonly used documentation method, the problem-oriented record, is useful for both students and expert clinicians. This paper or electronic format for documentation provides (1) an indexing system for easy retrieval of information, (2) checkpoints for self-evaluation of diagnostic and therapeutic judgments, and (3) a master problem list (client problems listed by number) to increase coordination of treatment plans among care providers. As the example on pp. 53–56 illustrates, it includes the problem, supporting data, and the plan of care. Each diagnosis is given a number and entered on the master problem list. Following the documentation of the admission nursing history and examination, the problem number, nursing diagnosis, clinical data, and plan are recorded. Guidelines for recording are on pp. 47–48. The same problem number is used for all subsequent charting on a specific nursing diagnosis. An example of recording a nursing history and examination, diagnoses, and treatment plans using a paper-based method is on pp. 49–56.

Subjective or objective data related to a disease or its treatment are documented in the client's record by number (e.g., #2 Diabetes mellitus). Relabeling of the medical problem to document the related nursing care is not necessary (e.g., alteration in glucose metabolism or alteration in cardiac output). In fact, relabeling in an indexing system leads to communication errors.

In some clinical settings without computerized records, a Kardex is used; nursing diagnoses (problem/etiology), treatments, and outcomes are listed on the Kardex. Medical diagnoses, doctor's orders, and any related nursing orders with regard to observation or monitoring, drugs, treatments, and standard diagnostic and treatment protocols are also placed on the Kardex. Additional nursing orders, such as those related to observation of disease or individualization of disease treatments, are also listed on the Kardex. These nursing orders are within the collaborative domain of nursing practice and do not alter the medical treatment of disease.

With these methods of documentation, the client's record will reflect nursing judgments, actions, and evaluations relative to nursing and medical diagnoses. The Kardex will serve as a quick reference to all client problems that require nursing attention.

PROBLEM-ORIENTED RECORDING GUIDELINES AND CHECKPOINTS

 # __ PROBLEM NUMBER AND LABEL—State clear, concise diagnostic label for the problem.

>Check below that S and O contain sufficient clinical data (diagnostic characteristics) for the problem.

>If insufficient information is available, record the possible diagnoses being considered or the major signs/ symptoms; continue assessment.

S: SUBJECTIVE DATA—List pertinent diagnostic indicators from verbal reports of individual or family.

>Record quotes when applicable.

>Check for consistency with objective data. Attempt to resolve incongruities or inconsistencies in data before recording.

O: OBJECTIVE DATA—List pertinent diagnostic indicators from direct observation and examination of individual or family, observations of context or milieu, and observational reports of other care providers, if pertinent.

>Check for measurement error, observer bias, and consistency with subjective data. Attempt to resolve incongruities or inconsistencies in data before recording.

Note: S and O data must provide sufficient diagnostic criteria to support problem and etiological factors. See individual
diagnosis pages to check defining characteristics.

A: ASSESSMENT—State etiological or related factors
contributing to the problem in # _____.

Use clear, concise terms.

Check that S and O data provide diagnostic characteristics for etiological factor(s). If information available is
insufficient to label etiological factors, record possible
factors being considered; continue assessment.

May include functional strengths pertinent to resolution
of the problem and any relevant prognostic statements.

High-risk diagnoses do not have etiological factors; the
risk factors recorded in S and O are the factors contributing to the high-risk state. They are the focus for
the plan of care.

P: PLAN—State projected outcome(s) and interventions.
Projected outcome(s): state concise, explicit, measurable, critical, attainable outcome(s) for the problem. State time of outcome attainment (e.g., discharge, 3 days, 4-week visit). If applicable, state a sequential set of outcomes and time frame.

Check that outcomes are specific to problem in # _____.

Check that date of outcome attainment is realistic. Consider etiological factors that may influence time for
outcome attainment.

Interventions: State intervention goal (optional). List concise nursing treatment orders. Include specific actions
(time and amount, if applicable).

Check that treatment orders are consistent with cause
stated in A and are specific to the individual client. If
there is a potential problem with no etiological factor,
check that treatment orders will reduce risk factors
specified under S and O.

Check that treatment orders have a high possibility for at-
taining outcome(s).

DOCUMENTATION: FORMAT AND EXAMPLE

If useful, classify plan by treatment orders (P-rx), diagnostic orders (P-dx), and teaching orders (P-ed).

EXAMPLE: NURSING HISTORY AND EXAMINATION

The following is an example of documentation of a nursing history and examination. Note that the first section has a few introductory sentences that alerts the reader to the age, sex, marital state, medical condition, and general appearance, race, and ethnic background when appropriate. Within this framework is information that suggests what norms are to be applied in judging whether a health pattern is functional, dysfunctional, or potentially dysfunctional.

NURSING HISTORY

First hospital admission of a 55-year-old, married, obese, administrator of a Spanish center. Sitting upright in bed, tense posture and expression. Five-year history of slightly elevated blood pressure. One-year PTA dizziness lasted 12 hours and started on medication; two other episodes relieved by rest. Seeks treatment at emergency room for dizziness and numbness of left arm.

Health-Perception–Health-Management Pattern: Viewed health as good until 1 year ago when diagnosed as having "high blood pressure." States job is "stressful, but the people need me." Had headaches for last 6 months and two episodes of dizziness, one at work and one at home lasting about 2 hours. Rested and symptoms went away. Delayed seeking care because was "too busy." Thought it was "overwork," not blood pressure. Discontinued blood pressure medication and visits to doctor about 6 months ago, "when blood pressure came down and I felt better"; states medicine caused impotence. Came to emergency room today because of left arm numbness and fear of stroke. Mother died of "stroke" 15 months ago. Concerned that he hasn't been taking care of himself and, "I need to learn about what to do." Wants to know "everything." Asked if it is okay to do some job-related paperwork if someone brought it in. Takes no medicine currently, except Alka-Seltzer and a laxative; doesn't smoke; drinks socially.

Nutritional-Metabolic Pattern: Sample diet related: MDR (minimum daily requirement) intake of protein, excess carbohydrate and fat; minimal high-roughage foods (fruits and vegetables), approximately 3 c coffee/day, fluid intake low, no history of lesions at mouth corners or mucous membranes; has gained weight gradually last 15 years. Some indigestion and heartburn after lunch attributed to days with multiple problems; takes Alka-Seltzer; dieting unsuccessful; problem is, "probably stress of job; I get home and eat a big supper and snacks in the evening"; no food dislikes. Takes lunch (sandwich and cake) to work and eats at desk; restaurants in area not good.

Elimination Pattern: Daily bowel movement pattern with two or three episodes of constipation/month lasting 2 days, hard stools, straining, and laxatives used. Attributes this pattern to his diet; knows he should eat better. Reports no problems voiding or in control of elimination.

Activity-Exercise Pattern: Spectator sports, uses car, minimal walking because of time schedule, sedentary job, considers self too old for exercise. Increasing fatigue last few weeks, less energy 2 months before admission; no self care deficit. Recreation consists of reading novels, watching television, dinner with other couples. Lives in first-floor apartment in city and drives 3/4 mile to work.

Sleep-Rest Pattern: Average 4 to 6 hours sleep/night, quiet atmosphere, own room with wife, double bed, uses bed board. Pre-sleep activities include watching television or completing paperwork from job; difficulty with sleep onset 1 month; awakens in morning many times thinking about job-related problems.

Cognitive-Perceptual Pattern: Sight corrected with glasses, changed 1 year ago; no change in hearing, taste, smell. No perceived change in memory, "I couldn't take it if I started losing my mind, like with a stroke." Learning ability: sees self as slower than in college, alert manner, grasps questions easily. Takes no sedatives, tranquilizers, other drugs. No headache at present.

Self-Perception–Self-Concept Pattern: Sees self as needing to do things well (job, father, husband); "Sometimes don't think I'm doing well with my family—having them live in this area—but in my job you have to be near when people need help." "It will be just great if I get sick and they have to take care of me, instead of me taking care of them."

Role-Relationship Pattern: Describes family as happy and understanding of his job commitments, wife formerly a social worker; kids "good; but I know we'll have trouble as Joe (10 years old) gets older"; "Maybe I should move us out of [lower socioeconomic area in city cited]." Ten-year-old assaulted 4 months ago; 14-year-old boy interested in sports and "keeps out of trouble, so far." Family usually "sits down together" to handle problems. Social relationships confined to "a few other couples"; finds this sufficient. Job demanding 9–10 hours/day, "always trying to get money to keep the center solvent" (assistant taking over while in hospital); enjoys job and helping people; coworkers are "good to work with." Wife states they are close; worried about husband's health; states he is more concerned with other people than himself; she admires him for this. Wife able to handle home responsibilities during hospitalization. States she and children had physical examination recently; no health problems; no elevation in blood pressure.

Sexuality-Reproductive Pattern: Two children; states was impotent when on BP medication. When "BP went down" stopped medications; potency returned. No problems perceived in sexual relationship.

Coping–Stress-Tolerance Pattern: Feels tense at work; has tried relaxation exercises with some alleviation; doesn't always have time. States the best way to deal with problems is to "attack them." Afraid of having a stroke and being dependent; "This thing today has really scared me." "I have too many things to think about at work and at home, and now this blood pressure thing." Life changes: father died 3 years ago; mother died of stroke 15 months ago. Took job at Spanish center 2 years ago to be near mother who "was getting old." Pleased he did this and feels good about it.

Value-Belief Pattern: "Life has been good to me"; feels deeply about "injustices in society" and wants to do something about them. States family is important to him. Religion (Catholic) important to him; would like to be active in church affairs.

EXAMINATION

Blood pressure ___205/118___   Temperature ___99.8___
Pulse rate __Regular and strong__   Respirations ___18___

NUTRITIONAL-METABOLIC PATTERN

Skin ___No area of redness over bony prominences; no lesions;___
dryness, discomfort from calluses on feet
Oral mucous membranes _____Moist, no lesions_____
Actual weight _230_ Reported weight _220_ Height __5'11"__

ACTIVITY-EXERCISE PATTERN

Gait ____Steady____ Posture _____Well balanced_____
Muscle tone, strength-coordination ___Hand grip firm, left and___
right; lifts legs; can pick up a pencil; tension in neck and shoulder
muscles
Range-of-motion (joints) Some tightness when bending forward
Prostheses/assistive devices _____None_____
Absence of body part _____No_____
Demonstrated ability for:
Feeding _____0_____   Grooming _____0____
Bathing _____0_____   General mobility ___0____
Toileting _____0_____   Dressing _____0____
(0 = full self care)

DOCUMENTATION: FORMAT AND EXAMPLE

COGNITIVE-PERCEPTUAL PATTERN

Perceptual Hears whisper Yes Reads newsprint With glasses
Language   English; grasps concrete and abstract ideas. Speech
clear; attention span good

SELF-PERCEPTION–SELF-CONCEPT PATTERN

General appearance _____ Well groomed, good hygiene _____
Nervous/relaxed   2 (scale of 1-5 with 1 as relaxed) Tense; some
relaxation during history taking

Eye contact _____ Yes _____ Attention span _____ Good _____
Assertive/passive   3 (on a scale of 1-5 with 1 being passive)

ROLE-RELATIONSHIP PATTERN

Interactions Communications with wife supportive; both somewhat
tense; children not present

PROBLEM LIST

1 Exogenous Obesity

S: Reports diet of excess carbohydrate and fat; big supper, evening snack, sandwich and cake at lunch, eats at desk.
Reports gradual weight gain last 15 years; considers self too
old for exercise; sedentary job; spectator sports, drives 3/4
mile to work. Reports 220 lbs.

O: 5'11", 230 lbs. Dryness, calluses on feet with discomfort when walking. Current diet order: 1200 calories

A: Caloric Intake–Energy Expenditure Imbalance. Reports
dieting unsuccessful in past; discomfort when walking may
reduce exercise.

  Discharge outcome: (1) Writes one week's 1200-calorie
  diet using calorie guide, (2) states how meal plan can
  be carried out within daily routine, and (3) states plan
  for increasing exercise and amount of weight loss to
  be achieved per month.

P: Discuss why dieting previously unsuccessful. Assess motivation, readiness, and current plans for weight loss; develop educational plan to achieve outcomes. Suggest podiatrist.

2 Intermittent Constipation Pattern

S: Daily bowel movement with two or three episodes of constipation per month; constipation lasts 2 days, hard stools, straining, laxatives used; attributes this to minimal high-roughage foods, low fluid intake; minimal walking, exercise; no constipation reported at present.

A: Dietary-Exercise Pattern

Discharge outcome: (1) Daily bowel movement without straining, and (2) states a plan for increasing fluid intake and high-fiber foods in diet.

P: Check qd bowel pattern in hospital. Provide supplementary fluids between meals. Integrate teaching of fluid and high-fiber food requirements into weight loss dietary teaching (see Problem #1).

3 Fear (dependency)

S: "Couldn't take it if started losing my mind, like with a stroke." "Just great if I get sick and they have to take care of me, instead of me taking care of them." States fear of stroke and becoming dependent—"this thing today has scared me"; mother died of stroke 15 months ago. States best way to deal with problems is to "attack them."

O: Neck and shoulder muscles tense

A: Perceived Risk of Stroke

Outcome, day 2: (1) Neck and shoulder muscles relaxed, and (2) identifies ways to reduce future risk of dependency (stroke).

P: Orient to environment and explain procedures (cognitive and sensory orientation). Back massage for relaxation q4h × 2 days. Allow to verbalize fears of dependency and channel thinking toward "attacking" risk factors; integrate discussion with dietary planning and conflict resolution.

4 Value Conflict

S: Feels deeply about injustices in society; wants to do something about them; head of Spanish center in inner city; enjoys job and helping people; coworkers good; job demanding, 9–10 hours/day; always trying to get money to keep Spanish center solvent; "job stressful, but people need me"; feels tense at work—tried relaxation; doesn't always have time to relax; 4 to 6 hours sleep/night, sleep onset difficulty 1 month, pre-sleep activities include job-related paperwork; awakens thinking about job-related problems.

Wife states he's more concerned with others than himself—admires him for this; kids "good, but know we'll have trouble as Joe gets older"; "maybe I should move"; 10-year-old assaulted 4 months ago; sees self as needing to do things well (job, father, husband); sometimes thinks "not doing well with my family—having them live in this area—but in my job you have to be near when people need help"; "I have too many things to think about at work, and at home, and now this blood pressure thing."

O: BP 205/118; 5-year history of essential hypertension.

A: Perceived Responsibilities (job and family, possibly self)

Discharge outcome: States plan for periodically assessing commitments/priorities in life.

P: Assess time constraints relative to valued activities (job, family, health management responsibilities). Help determine high-priority responsibilities (clarify values). Discuss possibility that time allocation to valued areas may resolve conflicts. Discuss value of health management so can continue to help others and realize goals. Consider nursing referral.

DOCUMENTATION: FORMAT AND EXAMPLE

5 High Risk Health-Management Deficit*

S: Delayed seeking care because "too busy"; attributed headaches and dizziness to overwork; stopped medicines and follow-up care "when BP went down"; states impotent on BP medicines.

O: BP 205/118; 5'11", 230 lbs.

A: May be motivated to improve health management at this time; states he wants to learn what to do.

Discharge outcome: States how daily routine will be adapted to implement health management plans (medication regimen, diet-exercise, bowel, and value-conflict management).

P: Assess motivation and readiness to improve health management; develop plan for learning management of hypertension, diet, exercise, elimination, and value conflict (the general plan of hypertensive and transient ischemic attack management can be reviewed until specific drugs, etc., are prescribed for discharge).

6 Hypertension with Evidence of Transient Ischemic Attack (medical diagnosis made and recorded by physician)

P: Zestril 200 mg bid; 1200-calorie diet with no added salt; BP q4h; medical orders: notify doctor if diastolic greater than 100, severe headache, dizziness. Observe for weakness in muscles of face or extremities and notify doctor (nursing order).

---

*It may be possible to cluster all other problems under Health-Management Deficit related to Perceived Responsibilities and Priorities. The care objective would be to help the client examine his values (priorities) and balancing job, family, and health-management responsibilities.

Diagnostic
Categories

Health-Perception–
Health-Management
Pattern

Health-Seeking Behaviors (Specify)

DEFINITION

Active seeking (by a person in stable health)* of ways to alter personal health habits and/or the environment to move toward a higher level of health

DEFINING CHARACTERISTICS

Diagnostic Cues

One or more of the following:

- Expressed or observed desire to seek a higher level of wellness
- Expressed or observed desire for increased control of health practices
- Expression of concern about current environmental conditions on health status
- Report or observation of unfamiliarity with wellness community resources
- Demonstrated or observed lack of knowledge in health promotion behaviors

*(Stable health status is defined as age-appropriate illness prevention measures achieved, client reports good or excellent health, and signs and symptoms of disease, if present, are controlled.)

HEALTH-PERCEPTION–HEALTH-MANAGEMENT PATTERN

Ineffective Health Maintenance (Specify)*

DEFINITION
Inability to identify basic health practices, manage own health, or seek help to maintain health

DEFINING CHARACTERISTICS
Diagnostic Cues

♦ Demonstrated lack of knowledge regarding basic health practices (inability to state this knowledge)

and/or

♦ Reported or observed inability to take responsibility for meeting basic health practices in any or all functional pattern areas

Supporting Cues

♦ History of lack of health-seeking behavior
♦ Expression of interest in improving health behaviors
♦ Demonstrated lack of adaptive behaviors to internal or external changes (see Impaired Adjustment)

ETIOLOGICAL OR RELATED FACTORS

♦ Unachieved developmental tasks
♦ Complete or partial lack of gross/fine motor skills
♦ Uncompensated perceptual-cognitive impairment (perception and judgment)
♦ Alteration in or lack of communication skills (written, verbal, gestural)
♦ Ineffective coping (individual or family)
♦ Disabling spiritual distress

Continues

Note: The definition specifies inability to manage; other diagnoses assume this ability is present. See Noncompliance, Health Management Deficit, Ineffective Therapeutic Regimen Management.

Ineffective Health Maintenance (Specify)—*cont'd*

+ Dysfunctional grieving
+ Reported or observed lack of material resources (equipment, finances, or other resources for health maintenance)
+ Reported or observed impairment of personal support system

HIGH-RISK POPULATIONS

+ Mental retardation
+ Cognitive impairment (e.g., severe head injury, Alzheimer's disease, dementia, and other mental disorders)
+ Sensory-motor impairment (e.g., hemiplegia, paraplegia)

Ineffective Therapeutic Regimen Management (Specify Area)*

DEFINITION

Pattern of regulating/integrating into daily living a program for treatment of illness and its sequelae that is not meeting specific health goals (specify medication, activity, other treatment regimens, or health promotion/disease prevention)

DEFINING CHARACTERISTICS

Diagnostic Cues

+ Report or observation that specific health goals are not met (specify goals)

and one of the following:

+ States did not take action to include treatment regimens in daily routines
+ States did not take action to reduce risk factors for progression of illness and sequelae

Supporting Cues

+ Choices about daily living ineffective for meeting goals of a treatment or prevention program (specify)
+ Acceleration (expected or unexpected) of illness symptoms
+ Verbalizes difficulty with regulation/integration of one or more prescribed regimens for treatment of illness or illness effects or for prevention of complications
+ Expresses desire to manage the treatment of illness or prevention of sequelae

Continues

---

*See also Noncompliance, Health Management Deficit, Altered Health Maintenance.

Ineffective Therapeutic Regimen Management (Specify Area)—*cont'd*

ETIOLOGICAL OR RELATED FACTORS

- Complexity of therapeutic regimen
- Low perceived seriousness
- Perceived low susceptibility
- Perceived barriers (specify)
- Perceived cost exceeds benefits
- Mistrust (specify; e.g., of regimen or health care personnel)
- Decisional conflict (specify)
- Economic difficulties
- Excessive demands (individual/family)
- Family conflict
- Family patterns of health care (specify)
- Inadequate cues to action (number/types)
- Knowledge deficit (specify)
- Social support deficits
- Complexity of health care system

HIGH-RISK POPULATIONS

- New treatment regimen
- Mental retardation
- Cognitive impairment (e.g., severe head injury, Alzheimer's disease, dementia, and other mental disorders)
- Sensory-motor impairment (e.g., hemiplegia, paraplegia)

Risk for Ineffective Therapeutic Regimen Management (Specify Area)*

DEFINITION

Presence of risk factors for difficulty in regulating/integrating a treatment or prevention program into daily living

RISK FACTORS

- Perceived low susceptibility/seriousness
- Perceived barriers (specify; e.g., value, cultural, or spiritual conflict)
- Perceived cost exceeds benefits
- Mistrust (specify; e.g., of regimen/health care personnel)
- Powerlessness
- Complexity of therapeutic regimen
- Decisional conflict (specify)
- Economic difficulties
- Excessive demands made on individual/family
- Family conflict
- Family patterns of health care (specify)
- Inadequate cues to action (number/types)
- Knowledge deficit (specify)
- Social support deficit
- Complexity of health care system
- Severe depression
- Impaired reality testing
- Uncompensated visual or hearing loss
- Uncompensated memory deficit
- Impaired mobility/coordination
- Activity intolerance
- Value conflict/priority setting
- Denial of illness

*See also Noncompliance, Health Management Deficit, Altered Health Maintenance.

Readiness for Enhanced Therapeutic Regimen Management

DEFINITION

Pattern of regulating and integrating into daily living a program for treatment of illness and its sequelae that is sufficient for meeting health-related goals and can be strengthened

DEFINING CHARACTERISTICS

- ◆ Expresses desire to manage the treatment of illness and prevention of sequelae
- ◆ Choices of daily living are appropriate for meeting the goals of treatment or prevention
- ◆ Expresses little or no difficulty with regulation/integration of one or more prescribed regimens for treatment of illness or prevention of complications
- ◆ Describes reduction of risk factors for progression of illness and sequelae
- ◆ No unexpected acceleration of illness symptoms

Effective Therapeutic Regimen Management (Specify Area)

DEFINITION

Satisfactory pattern of regulating and integrating into daily living a program for treatment of illness and its sequelae

DEFINING CHARACTERISTICS

- Appropriate choices of daily activities for meeting the goals of a treatment or prevention program
- Illness symptoms are within a normal range of expectation
- Verbalized desire to manage the treatment of illness and prevention of sequelae
- Verbalized intent to reduce risk factors for progression of illness and sequelae

Ineffective Family Therapeutic Regimen Management (Specify Area)*

DEFINITION

Pattern of regulating and integrating into family processes a program for treatment of illness and the sequelae of illness that is unsatisfactory for meeting specific health goals

DEFINING CHARACTERISTICS

- Inappropriate family activities for meeting the goals of a treatment or prevention program
- Acceleration of illness symptoms of a family member
- Lack of attention to illness and its sequelae
- Verbalized desire to manage the treatment of illness and prevention of the sequelae
- Verbalized difficulty with regulation/integration of one or more effects or prevention of complication
- Verbalizes that family did not take action to reduce risk factors for progression of illness and sequelae

ETIOLOGICAL OR RELATED FACTORS

- Complexity of health care system
- Complexity of therapeutic regimen
- Decisional conflicts
- Economic difficulties
- Excessive demands made on individual or family
- Family conflict

*See also Noncompliance, Health Management Deficit, Ineffective Health Maintenance.

Ineffective Community Therapeutic Regimen Management (Specify Area)*

DEFINITION

Pattern of regulating and integrating into community processes programs for treatment of illness and sequelae of illness that are unsatisfactory for meeting health-related goals

DEFINING CHARACTERISTICS

- ♦ Deficits in accountability of persons and programs for illness care of aggregates (primary, secondary, and tertiary prevention)
- ♦ Deficits in advocates for aggregates
- ♦ Illness symptoms above the norm expected for the number and type of population
- ♦ Number of health care resources are insufficient or unavailable for the prevalence of illness(es)
- ♦ Unexpected acceleration of illness(es)

*See also Health Management Deficit, Ineffective Health Maintenance.

Health-Management Deficit (Specify Area)

DEFINITION

Inability to manage activities related to health promotion
and/or disease or disability prevention/progression (Specify
drug or treatment regimen, dietary prescription, observation
and reporting of symptoms, follow-up care of disease, health
promotion, and disease prevention.)

DEFINING CHARACTERISTICS

Diagnostic Cues

One or more of the following:
  * Report or observation of inability to manage treatment
    regimen
  * Report or observation of inability to manage mental
    or physical health-promotion activities specific to age
    and developmental stage
  * Report or observation of insufficient actions to prevent
    diseases or disabilities that pose a risk to the
    individual or family

ETIOLOGICAL OR RELATED FACTORS

  * Knowledge deficit (specify area)
  * Priority setting (values)
  * Parental care priorities
  * Severe depression
  * Impaired reality testing
  * Uncompensated memory deficit
  * Impaired mobility (levels II through IV)
  * Uncompensated impaired coordination
  * Uncompensated perceptual or cognitive impairment
  * Activity intolerance (level III or IV)

HIGH-RISK POPULATIONS

- ◆ New and/or complex treatment regimen
- ◆ Mental retardation
- ◆ Cognitive impairment (e.g., severe head injury, Alzheimer's disease, dementia, and other mental disorders)
- ◆ Sensory-motor impairment (e.g., hemiplegia, paraplegia)

Risk for Health-Management Deficit (Specify Area)

DEFINITION

Presence of risk factors for inability to manage activities related to health promotion and/or disease or disability prevention (specify drug or treatment regimen, dietary prescription, observation and reporting of symptoms, follow-up care of disease, health promotion, disease prevention)

RISK FACTORS

+ Priority setting, knowledge, comprehension, and/or motor skills needed for continuing treatment of disease exceed actual or potential competencies
+ Priority setting, knowledge, comprehension, and/or motor skills required for specific health promotion and disease prevention activities exceed actual or potential competencies
+ Activity intolerance (level IV)
+ Uncompensated perceptual or cognitive impairment
+ Uncompensated impaired coordination
+ Impaired mobility (levels II through IV)
+ Uncompensated short-term memory deficit
+ Uncompensated visual or hearing loss
+ Impaired reality testing
+ Severe depression

Noncompliance (Specify Area)

DEFINITION

Nonadherence to a therapeutic recommendation following informed decision and expressed intention to attain therapeutic goals (specify drug or treatment regimen, dietary prescription, observation and reporting of symptoms, follow-up care, health-promoting behaviors)

DEFINING CHARACTERISTICS

Diagnostic Cues

One or more of the following:

- Direct observation of noncompliance or statements by client or significant others describing behaviors indicating failure to adhere
- Objective tests revealing nonadherence (physiological measures, detection of markers)

Supporting Cues

- Evidence of development of complications
- Evidence of exacerbation of symptoms
- Failure to keep appointments
- Failure to progress (resolve problem)

ETIOLOGICAL OR RELATED FACTORS

- Value, health beliefs, cultural, or spiritual conflict
- Knowledge or skill deficit (developmental abilities)
- Perceived therapeutic ineffectiveness
- Perceived nonsusceptibility or invulnerability
- Denial of illness
- Family pattern disruption

Continues

Noncompliance (Specify Area)—*cont'd*

+ Low motivation
+ Satisfaction with care, credibility, continuity of provider, access, convenience of care, and client-provider relationship

HIGH-RISK POPULATIONS

+ New and/or complex treatment regimen (duration, cost, or complexity)

Risk for Noncompliance (Specify Area)

DEFINITION

Presence of risk factors for nonadherence to the therapeutic recommendations following informed decision and expressed intention to adhere or to attain therapeutic goals

RISK FACTORS

- Denial of illness
- Perceived ineffectiveness of recommended practices
- Perceived lack of seriousness of problem or risk factors
- Perceived lack of susceptibility
- Insufficient knowledge or skills (therapeutic recommendations)
- Absence of a plan for integrating therapeutic recommendations into daily routines
- New and/or complex treatment regimen
- Lack of support systems (supportive others)
- History of noncompliance with aspects of therapeutic regimen

Risk for Infection (Specify Type and Area)

DEFINITION

Presence of increased risk for invasion by pathogenic organisms (specify respiratory, urinary tract, skin)

RISK FACTORS

- Tissue destruction (surgical wound, traumatized tissues, invasive procedure, bites, burns)
- Skin breakdown (e.g., pressure ulceration)
- Stasis of body fluids or secretions (e.g., bladder, lungs, sinuses)
- Immunosuppression (e.g., chemotherapy, steroids, stress, disease)
- Inadequate acquired immunity
- Increased environmental exposure to pathogens (specify type)
- Inadequate secondary defenses: leukopenia (e.g., radiation, chemotherapy)
- Decreased hemoglobin and oxygen transport, suppressed inflammatory response
- Chronic disease with debilitation
- Malnutrition; hyperglycemia
- Change in normal flora (antibiotic, antiviral, antifungal medicines)
- Decrease in ciliary action
- Insufficient knowledge to avoid exposure to pathogens
- Warm, moist, dark areas (e.g., skin folds)
- Rupture of amniotic membranes
- Altered peristalsis
- Change in pH of secretions
- Presence of stressors
- Radiation therapy

Risk for Injury (Trauma)

DEFINITION

Presence of risk factors for trauma to the body

RISK FACTORS

Cognitive Factors

- Excess alcohol-ingestion pattern
- Impaired judgment (disease, drugs, impaired reality testing, risk-taking behavior)
- Sensory-perceptual loss or deterioration (temperature, touch, position sense, vision, hearing)
- Disorientation
- Unfamiliar setting
- Inability to use call light; inappropriate call-for-aid mechanisms

Mobility Factors

- Impaired mobility (specify; e.g., muscle weakness, paralysis, balancing difficulties, coordination)
- Report of dizziness, vertigo, syncope

Safety Factors

- Smoking in bed or near oxygen
- Lack of safety precautions, safety education
- History of previous trauma, accidental injury (falling, car accidents)
- Entering unlighted rooms
- Use of cracked dishware or glasses
- Use of thin or worn potholders or mitts
- Driving mechanically unsafe vehicles; driving after consuming alcoholic beverages, drugs

Continues

Risk for Injury (Trauma)—*cont'd*

- Driving at excessive speeds or without necessary visual aids
- Nonuse or misuse of seat restraints, headgear for cyclists and passengers
- Overexposure to sun or sun lamps

Child Supervision

- Bathing in very hot water; unsupervised bathing of young children
- Experimenting with chemicals or gasoline; contact with acid or alkali
- Play or work near vehicle pathways (driveways, roads, railroad tracks)
- Children playing with matches, candles, cigarettes, fireworks, gunpowder, sharp-edged toys
- Children riding in front seat of automobile; unrestrained babies riding in car
- Children playing without gates at top of stairs
- Highly flammable children's toys or clothing

Environment

- Sliding on coarse bed linen and struggling within bed restraints
- High beds
- Slippery, littered, or obstructed floors, stairs, walkways (wet, highly waxed, snow, ice)
- Unanchored rugs, unsturdy or absent stair rails; unsteady ladders or chairs
- Bathtub without hand grips or antislip equipment
- Unanchored electric wires
- Knives stored uncovered
- Guns or ammunition stored in unlocked area

HEALTH-PERCEPTION–HEALTH-MANAGEMENT PATTERN

- Large icicles hanging from roof
- Overloaded fuse boxes or electrical outlets; faulty electrical plugs, frayed wires; defective appliances
- Pot handles facing toward front of stove
- Potential igniting gas leaks; delayed lighting of fast burner or oven; grease waste collected on stoves
- High-crime neighborhood, unsafe roads or road-crossing conditions
- Exposure to dangerous machinery, contact with rapidly moving machinery, industrial belts, pulleys
- Inadequately stored combustible or corrosive materials (matches, oily rags, lye)
- Unsafe window protection in homes with young children
- Insufficient finances to purchase safety equipment or make repairs

Risk for Falls

DEFINITION
Increased susceptibility for falling that may cause physical harm

RISK FACTORS

General Factors: Children

- Less than 2 years of age
- Male gender when less than 1 year of age
- Lack of auto restraints
- Lack of gate on stairs and window guards
- Bed located near window
- Unattended infant on bed, changing table, or sofa
- Lack of parental supervision

General Factors: Adult

- History of falls
- Wheelchair use
- Age 65 or over
- Female (if elderly)
- Lives alone
- Lower limb prosthesis, assistive devices (e.g., walker, cane)

Physiological Factors

- Presence of acute illness
- Postoperative conditions
- Visual or hearing difficulties
- Arthritis
- Orthostatic hypotension
- Sleeplessness
- Feeling faint when turning or extending neck
- Anemia, vascular disease

HEALTH-PERCEPTION–HEALTH-MANAGEMENT PATTERN

- Postprandial blood sugar change
- Diarrhea
- Decreased lower extremity strength
- Foot problems (e.g., neuropathy)
- Impaired physical mobility and balance
- Gait disturbance
- Proprioceptive deficits (e.g., unilateral neglect)

Cognitive Factors

- Diminished mental status (e.g., confusion, delirium, impaired reality testing)

Chemical Factors

- Antihypertensive agents, diuretics (ACE inhibitors)
- Tricyclic antidepressants, antianxiety agents, hypnotics, tranquilizers
- Alcohol use
- Narcotics

Environmental Factors

- Restraints
- Weather conditions (e.g., ice, wet floors)
- Throw/scatter rugs
- Cluttered environment
- Unfamiliar dimly lit room
- No antislip material in bathroom and shower

Risk for Perioperative-Positioning Injury

DEFINITION

Presence of risk factors for injury as a result of the environmental conditions found in the perioperative setting

RISK FACTORS

- Sensory/perceptual disturbances caused by anesthesia
- Disorientation
- Immobilization
- Muscle weakness
- Obesity
- Emaciation
- Edema

Risk for Poisoning

DEFINITION
Presence of risk factors for accidental exposure to (or ingestion of) drugs or dangerous products in doses sufficient to cause poisoning

RISK FACTORS
Environmental Factors

- Flaking, peeling paint or plaster in presence of young children
- Dangerous products placed or stored within reach of children or confused persons
- Medicines stored in unlocked cabinets accessible to children or confused persons
- Large supplies of drugs in the house
- Availability of illicit drug potentially contaminated by poisonous additives
- Chemical contamination of food or water
- Unprotected contact with heavy metals or chemicals
- Paint, lacquer, etc., in poorly ventilated areas or without effective protection
- Presence of poisonous vegetation
- Presence of atmospheric pollution

Personal Factors

- Reduced vision
- Cognitive impairment or emotional difficulties
- Occupational setting without adequate safeguards
- Lack of safety or drug education
- Insufficient finances

Risk for Suffocation

DEFINITION

Presence of risk factors for accidental interruption in air available for inhalation

RISK FACTORS

Personal Factors

- Reduced olfactory sensation
- Cognitive impairment or emotional difficulties
- Mobility impairment (bed mobility or ambulation)
- Knowledge deficit (safety education)
- Eating large mouthfuls of food

Safety Factors

- Vehicle warming in a closed garage
- Pillow placed in an infant's crib
- Propped bottle placed in an infant's crib
- Pacifier hung around an infant's neck
- Children playing in plastic bags, inserting small objects into their mouths or noses
- Discarded or unused refrigerators or freezers without removed doors
- Children left unattended in bathtubs or pools
- Household gas leaks
- Use of fuel-burning heaters not vented to the outside

Ineffective Protection (Specify)

DEFINITION

Decreased ability to guard self from internal or external
threats such as illness or injury

DEFINING CHARACTERISTICS

Diagnostic Cues

One or more of the following:
- Deficient immunity
- Impaired healing
- Altered clotting
- Maladaptive stress response
- Neurosensory alterations; disorientation

Supporting Cues

- Chilling, perspiring
- Dyspnea, cough
- Itching
- Restlessness
- Insomnia, fatigue, anorexia, weakness
- Immobility
- Pressure ulcers

ETIOLOGICAL OR RELATED FACTORS

- Alcohol abuse
- Inadequate nutrition

HIGH-RISK POPULATIONS

- Abnormal blood profiles (leukopenia,
  thrombocytopenia, anemia, coagulation)
- Drug therapies (antineoplastic, corticosteroid,
  immune, anticoagulant, thrombolytic)
- Treatments (surgery, radiation, cancer, immune
  disorders)

Disturbed Energy Field

DEFINITION

Disruption of the flow of energy surrounding a person's being that results in a disharmony of the body, mind, and/or spirit

DEFINING CHARACTERISTICS

- Perceptions of changes in patterns of energy flow such as:
  - Movement (wave, spike, tingling, dense, flowing)
  - Sounds (tone/words)
  - Temperature change (warmth/coolness)
  - Disruption of the field (deficit, vacant/hole/spike/bulge, obstruction, congestion, diminished flow in energy field)
  - Visual changes (image/color)

ETIOLOGICAL OR RELATED FACTORS

Slowing or blocking of energy flows secondary to one or more of the following:

Pathophysiologic Factors

- Illness
- Pregnancy
- Injury

Treatment-Related Factors

- Immobility
- Labor and delivery
- Perioperative experience
- Chemotherapy

HEALTH-PERCEPTION–HEALTH-MANAGEMENT PATTERN

Situational Factors

♦ Pain
♦ Fear
♦ Anxiety
♦ Grieving

Maturational Factors

♦ Age-related developmental crises

NOTES

NOTES

NOTES

Nutritional-Metabolic Pattern

Adult Failure to Thrive*

DEFINITION

Progressive functional deterioration of a physical and cognitive nature (associated with multisystem disease that is no longer responsive to medical interventions; condition may respond to psychosocial nursing interventions when diagnosed early)

DEFINING CHARACTERISTICS

+ Anorexia (loss of appetite); does not eat meals when offered; states does not have an appetite, not hungry, or "I don't want to eat"
+ Inadequate nutritional intake, eating less than body requirements; consumes minimal to none of food at most meals (i.e., consumes less than 75% of normal requirements at each, or most, meals)
+ Weight loss (decreased body mass from baseline weight, i.e., 5% unintentional weight loss in 1 month, 10% unintentional weight loss in 6 months)
+ Physical decline (decline in bodily function with evidence of fatigue, dehydration, incontinence of bowel and bladder; frequent exacerbation of chronic health problems such as congestive heart failure, pneumonia, urinary tract infections)
+ Cognitive decline (decline in mental processing, as evidenced by problems with responding appropriately to environmental stimuli; demonstrates difficulty in reasoning, decision making, judgment, memory, concentration, decreased perception)

---

*This diagnosis meets the criteria for a syndrome.

- Decreased social skills/social withdrawal (noticeable decrease in attempts to form or participate in cooperative and interdependent relationships, e.g., decreased verbal communication with staff, family, friends; decreased participation in activities of daily living and activities that the person once enjoyed)
- Self-care deficit (e.g., no longer looks after or takes charge of physical cleanliness or appearance; difficulty performing simple self-care tasks; neglects home environment and/or financial responsibilities. Apathy as evidenced by lack of observable feeling or emotion in terms of normal activities of daily living and environment)
- Depression (altered mood state): Expresses feeling "depressed"

and/or one or more of the following:

- Feelings of sadness, low in spirits and mood
- Loss of interest in pleasurable outlets such as food, sex, work, friends, family, hobbies, or entertainment
- Apathy, lethargy, fatigue
- Decreased motivation in performing activities of daily living
- Appears depressed (e.g., spends much of the time in bed with face to wall), verbalizes desire for death
- Helplessness

HIGH-RISK POPULATIONS

- Primarily seen in adult/elderly (1) with multisystem disease that is no longer responsive to medical interventions (2) who are coping with the ensuing problems, and (3) have a remarkably diminished ability to manage own care

Imbalanced Nutrition: More Than Body Requirements or *Exogenous Obesity*

DEFINITION
Intake of nutrients exceeds metabolic need

DEFINING CHARACTERISTICS
Diagnostic Cues
- Triceps skin fold greater than 15 mm in men and 25 mm in women
- Body mass index 30 or higher (obesity); 25 or more (overweight)
- Weight greater than 20% over ideal for height and frame (obesity); weight 10% to 20% over ideal for height and frame (overweight)
- Reported intake greater than RDA (recommended daily allowance)

Supporting Cues
- Pale conjunctiva and mucous membranes

ETIOLOGICAL OR RELATED FACTORS
- Food intake–energy expenditure imbalance
- Dysfunctional eating patterns (reported or observed):
  - Pairing food with other activities
  - Concentrating food intake at end of day
  - Eating in response to external cues (time of day, social situation)
  - Eating in response to internal cues other than hunger (anxiety, depression)
- Sedentary activity level (relative to caloric intake)
- Knowledge deficit (nutritional requirements)

HIGH-RISK POPULATIONS

- History of childhood obesity/overweight
- Emotional disorders, life stress
- Enforced sedentary lifestyle (e.g., wheelchair bound)

Risk for Imbalanced Nutrition: More Than Body Requirements or *Risk for Obesity*

DEFINITION

Presence of risk factors for intake of nutrients that exceeds metabolic need

RISK FACTORS

- ◆ Dysfunctional eating patterns:
  - ◆ Pairing food with other activities
  - ◆ Concentrating food intake at end of day
  - ◆ Eating in response to external cues (time of day, social situation)
  - ◆ Eating in response to internal cues (anxiety, depression)
- ◆ Sedentary activity level
- ◆ Reported or observed obesity in one or both parents; hereditary predisposition
- ◆ Rapid transition across growth percentiles in infants or children
- ◆ Excessive intake relative to energy expenditure during late gestational life, early infancy, and adolescence
- ◆ Dysfunctional psychological conditioning in response to food (use of food as reward or comfort measure)
- ◆ Frequent, closely spaced pregnancies; reported or observed higher baseline at beginning of pregnancy
- ◆ Low financial resources (selection of lower-cost, high-caloric foods)

Imbalanced Nutrition: Less Than Body Requirements or *Nutritional Deficit (Specify Type)*

DEFINITION

Insufficient intake of nutrients to meet metabolic needs

DEFINING CHARACTERISTICS

Diagnostic Cues

+ Body mass index 18 or less
+ Weight loss (with or without adequate intake); 20% or more under ideal body weight
+ Reported or observed food intake less than recommended minimum daily requirement

Supporting Cues

+ Fatigue
+ Capillary fragility
+ Pale conjunctiva and mucous membranes
+ Excessive hair loss, poor muscle tone
+ Hyperactive bowel sounds, abdominal cramping, pain
+ Diarrhea and/or steatorrhea

ETIOLOGICAL OR RELATED FACTORS

+ Buccal cavity discomfort or pain
+ Pain with mastication (dental caries)
+ Altered or loss of taste sensation
+ Inability to prepare or obtain food
+ Diarrhea, steatorrhea
+ Knowledge deficit (daily requirements)
+ Financial limitations
+ Social isolation
+ Anorexia, setophobia, early satiety

Continues

Imbalanced Nutrition: Less Than Body Requirements or *Nutritional Deficit (Specify Type)—cont'd*

- ♦ Chemical dependency
- ♦ Emotional stress
- ♦ Food faddism, dieting practices
- ♦ Muscle weakness (mastication, swallowing)

HIGH-RISK POPULATIONS

- ♦ Hypermetabolic or catabolic states
- ♦ Absorptive disorders
- ♦ Low income

Readiness for Enhanced Nutrition

DEFINITION

Pattern of nutrient intake that is sufficient for meeting metabolic needs and can be strengthened

DEFINING CHARACTERISTICS

+ Expresses desire/willingness to enhance nutrition
+ Eats regularly
+ Consumes adequate food and fluid
+ Expresses knowledge of health food and fluid choices
+ Follows appropriate standard for types of intake (e.g., food pyramid, Diabetic Association Guidelines)
+ Prepares and stores food and fluids safely
+ Attitude toward eating and drinking is congruent with health goals

Interrupted Breastfeeding

DEFINITION

Break in continuity of breastfeeding process as a result of inability or inadvisability to put baby to breast for feeding

DEFINING CHARACTERISTICS

Diagnostic Cues

+ Infant does not receive nourishment at the breast for some or all feedings
+ Presence of factors interfering with maternal desire to maintain lactation and provide (or eventually provide) her breast milk for infant's nutritional needs (specify)

ETIOLOGICAL OR RELATED FACTORS

+ Knowledge deficit (expression and storage of breast milk)
+ Mother-infant separation (e.g., maternal employment)
+ Contraindications to breastfeeding (e.g., drugs, true breast milk jaundice)
+ Need to abruptly wean infant (e.g., maternal or infant illness)

HIGH RISK POPULATIONS

+ Prematurity

Ineffective Breastfeeding

DEFINITION

Dissatisfaction or difficulty with the breastfeeding process experienced by mother or infant/child

DEFINING CHARACTERISTICS

Diagnostic Cues

Report or observation of one or more of the following behavioral patterns:

+ Actual or perceived inadequate milk supply
+ Infant inability to attach to maternal breast correctly
+ No observable signs of oxytocin release
+ Observable signs of inadequate infant intake
+ Nonsustained or insufficient opportunity for suckling at the breast
+ Insufficient emptying of each breast per feeding
+ Persistence of sore nipples beyond the first week of breastfeeding
+ Infant exhibiting fussiness and crying within first hour after breastfeeding; unresponsive to comfort measures
+ Infant arching and crying at the breast; infant resisting latching on

Supporting Cues

+ Previous history of breastfeeding failure
+ Report of unsatisfactory breastfeeding process

ETIOLOGICAL OR RELATED FACTORS

+ Knowledge deficit (breastfeeding)
+ Interrupted breastfeeding
+ Maternal anxiety; maternal ambivalence
+ Prematurity or infant anomaly

Continues

Ineffective Breastfeeding—*cont'd*

- Maternal breast anomaly; previous breast surgery
- Infant supplemental feedings with artificial nipple
- Poor infant sucking reflex
- Nonsupportive partner or family

HIGH-RISK POPULATIONS

- Previous history of breastfeeding failure
- Infant anomaly

Effective Breastfeeding*

DEFINITION

Mother-infant dyad/family exhibits adequate proficiency and satisfaction with breastfeeding process

DEFINING CHARACTERISTICS

Diagnostic Cues

- Mother is able to position infant at breast to promote a successful latch-on response
- Infant is content after feeding
- Appropriate infant weight patterns for age
- Regular and sustained suckling/swallowing at the breast
- Effective mother-infant communication patterns (infant cues; maternal interpretation and response)

Supporting Cues

- Signs or symptoms of oxytocin release (let-down or milk ejection reflex)
- Adequate infant elimination patterns for age
- Eagerness of infant to nurse
- Maternal verbalization of satisfaction with the breastfeeding process
- Basic breastfeeding knowledge
- Normal breast structure
- Normal infant oral structure
- Infant gestational age greater than 34 weeks
- Presence of support sources
- Maternal confidence

*This diagnostic category does not represent a problem or risk. As with other healthy states or processes, periodic assessment is advisable.

Ineffective Infant Feeding Pattern*

DEFINITION

Impaired ability to suck or coordinate the suck-swallow response

DEFINING CHARACTERISTICS

Diagnostic Cues

+ Inability to initiate or sustain an effective suck
+ Inability to coordinate sucking, swallowing, and breathing

HIGH-RISK POPULATIONS

+ Prematurity
+ Neurological impairment/delay (specify)
+ Prolonged NPO
+ Anatomic abnormality (specify e.g., cleft lip, cleft palate)
+ Oral hypersensitivity

*This condition is frequently a focus for intervention (i.e., an etiological/related factor).

Impaired Swallowing (Uncompensated)

DEFINITION
Decreased ability to voluntarily pass fluids and/or solids from the mouth to the stomach

DEFINING CHARACTERISTICS
Diagnostic Cues

+ Observed or reported difficulty in swallowing:
    + Coughing/choking when swallowing
    + Stasis of food in oral cavity (cheek pocket)

Supporting Cues

+ Evidence of aspiration
+ Unsatisfactory breastfeeding process
+ Nonsustained suckling at the breast

ETIOLOGICAL OR RELATED FACTORS

+ Uncompensated perceptual motor weakness/loss
+ Fatigue
+ Reddened, irritated oropharyngeal cavity
+ Limited awareness

HIGH-RISK POPULATIONS

+ Neuromuscular or perceptual impairment (e.g., decreased or absent gag reflex, decreased strength or excursion of muscles involved in mastication, facial paralysis)
+ Mechanical obstruction (e.g., edema, tracheostomy tube, tumor)

Nausea

DEFINITION

Unpleasant, wavelike sensation in the back of the throat, epigastrium, or throughout the abdomen, that may or may not lead to vomiting

DEFINING CHARACTERISTICS

Diagnostic Cues

+ Verbal report of "nauseated" or "sick to stomach"
+ Increased salivation, swallowing
+ Gagging sensation

Supporting Cues

+ Accompanied by pallor, cold and clammy skin; tachycardia, gastric stasis, and/or diarrhea

ETIOLOGICAL OR RELATED FACTORS

+ Gastrointestinal system irritation
+ Stimulation of neuropharmacologic mechanisms

HIGH-RISK POPULATIONS

+ Chemotherapy, radiotherapy
+ Postsurgical anesthesia
+ Toxins
+ Biochemical disorders (e.g., uremia, ketoacidosis)
+ Pregnancy
+ Pharmaceuticals (antiviral for HIV, aspirin, opioids)

Risk for Aspiration

DEFINITION

Risk for entry of gastrointestinal secretions, oropharyngeal secretions, or solids or fluids into tracheobronchial passages

RISK FACTORS

- Impaired swallowing
- Reduced level of consciousness
- Depressed cough and gag reflexes
- Situations hindering elevation of upper body
- Incomplete lower esophageal sphincter
- Presence of tracheostomy or endotracheal tube
- Gastrointestinal tubes
- Tube feedings
- Medication administration
- Increased intragastric pressure
- Increased gastric residual
- Decreased gastrointestinal motility
- Delayed gastric emptying
- Facial, neck, or oral surgery
- Facial, neck, or oral trauma
- Wired jaws
- Seizures
- Vomiting

NUTRITIONAL-METABOLIC PATTERN

Impaired Oral Mucous Membrane (Specify Impairment)

DEFINITION

Disruption of lips and soft tissue in the oral cavity

DEFINING CHARACTERISTICS

- Stomatitis
- Membrane hyperemia ("beefy red")
- Halitosis
- Edema (gingival or mucosal)
- Bleeding
- Gingival hyperplasia, fissures, cheilitis
- Self-report of bad, diminished, or absent taste
- Self-report of bad taste; difficulty eating or swallowing
- Difficult speech (dysarthria)
- Purulent drainage or exudate
- Oral pain/discomfort
- Smooth atrophic, sensitive tongue; geographic tongue
- Dry mouth (xerostomia)
- Mucosal denudation
- Oral lesions or ulceration (white patches/plaques, spongy patches or white, curdlike exudate; vesicles, nodules, or papules)
- Gingival recession (pockets deeper than 4 mm)
- Gingival or mucosal pallor
- Enlarged tonsils beyond what is developmentally appropriate
- Red or bluish masses, e.g., hemangioma
- Desquamation

NUTRITIONAL-METABOLIC PATTERN

ETIOLOGICAL OR RELATED FACTORS

- Ineffective oral hygiene practices
- Chemical irritants (e.g., alcohol, tobacco, acidic foods, regular use of inhalers)
- Dehydration (excessive fluid loss, e.g., sweating, vomiting)
- Mouth breathing
- Malnutrition or vitamin deficiency
- Stress, depression
- Immunocompromised
- Medication side effects
- Lack of or decreased salivation
- Barriers to oral self-care
- Barriers to professional care
- Poorly fitting dental prostheses
- Mechanical factors: tubes (endotracheal/nasogastric), ill-fitting dentures, braces, biting/chewing

HIGH-RISK POPULATIONS

- Oral surgery, trauma
- Cleft lip or palate
- Radiation therapy (head/neck/mouth) or chemotherapy
- Pathology (e.g., cancer, infection, periodontal disease, decreased platelets)
- Loss of supportive oral structures
- Aging-related loss of connective, adipose, or bone tissue
- Diminished hormone levels (women)

Impaired Dentition

DEFINITION
Disruption in tooth development/eruption patterns or structural integrity of individual teeth

DEFINING CHARACTERISTICS
- Missing or loose teeth or complete absence of teeth
- Toothache
- Sensitivity to heat or cold
- Excessive plaque
- Crown or root caries
- Halitosis
- Tooth enamel discoloration
- Excessive calculus
- Worn down or abraded teeth
- Tooth fracture(s)
- Erosion of enamel
- Asymmetrical facial expression
- Incomplete eruption for age (primary or permanent teeth)
- Malocclusion or tooth misalignment
- Premature loss of primary teeth

ETIOLOGICAL OR RELATED FACTORS
- Ineffective oral hygiene
- Barriers to self-care (specify)
- Access or economic barriers to professional care
- Nutritional deficits, dietary habits
- Premature loss of primary teeth
- Excessive intake of fluorides
- Chronic vomiting
- Chronic use of tobacco, coffee or tea, red wine
- Knowledge deficit (dental health)
- Excessive use of abrasive cleaning agents; bruxism

Risk for Imbalanced Fluid Volume

DEFINITION

Risk for decrease, increase, or rapid shift among intravascular, interstitial, and/or intracellular fluid compartments

RISK FACTORS

- Major invasive procedure
- Other risk factors to be determined

Excess Fluid Volume*

DEFINITION

Increased isotonic fluid retention

DEFINING CHARACTERISTICS

- Weight gain over short period
- Intake exceeds output
- Altered electrolytes
- Increased central venous pressure
- Third heart sound (S_3 gallop)
- Blood pressure changes
- Abnormal breath sounds (rales or crackles)
- Dyspnea (shortness of breath), orthopnea
- Pleural effusion
- Pulmonary congestion, pulmonary artery pressure changes
- Hepatic congestion, positive hepatojugular reflex
- Anasarca, oliguria, specific gravity changes
- Decreased blood urea nitrogen; azotemia
- Decreased hemoglobin and hematocrit
- Central venous pressure >11 cm water
- Change in mental status (restlessness)

ETIOLOGICAL OR RELATED FACTORS

- Excess sodium intake (e.g., excess isotonic intravenous fluids)
- Excess fluid intake
- Compromised regulatory mechanism

HIGH-RISK POPULATIONS

- Renal failure
- Congestive heart failure
- Cirrhosis
- Cushing's syndrome

*If diagnosed, refer for medical evaluation.

Deficient Fluid Volume*

DEFINITION

Decreased intravascular, interstitial, and/or intracellular fluid below normal range for individual (this refers to dehydration—water loss alone without change in sodium)

DEFINING CHARACTERISTICS

- Thirst
- Sudden weight loss (except in third spacing)
- Decreased blood pressure
- Increased pulse rate
- Decreased urine output (oliguria)
- Increased urine concentration, increased specific gravity
- Increased body temperature
- Decreased pulse volume or pressure
- Change in mental state
- Dry skin and mucous membranes
- Decreased skin turgor
- Weakness
- Decreased venous filling
- Elevated hematocrit

ETIOLOGICAL OR RELATED FACTORS

- Active fluid volume loss (normal routes, tubes; diarrhea)
- Failure of regulatory mechanisms

HIGH-RISK POPULATIONS

- Conditions affecting access to fluids
- Conditions affecting absorption of fluids
- Hypermetabolic states (hyperthermia, etc.)
- Extremes of age/weight

*If diagnosed, refer for medical evaluation.

Risk for Deficient Fluid Volume

DEFINITION

Presence of risk factors for decrease in body fluid (vascular, cellular, or intracellular dehydration)

RISK FACTORS

- Impaired ability to take in fluids
- Excessive loss of fluid through normal routes (describe; e.g., diarrhea)
- Loss of fluid through abnormal routes (describe; e.g., indwelling tubes)
- Excessive insensible loss
- Deviations affecting access to fluids, intake of fluids, or absorption of fluids (e.g., physical immobility, unconsciousness)
- Medications (e.g., diuretics)
- Factors influencing fluid requirements (e.g., hypermetabolic states; hyperthermia; dry, hot environment)
- Extremes of age
- Hyperthermia
- Knowledge deficit (fluid volume needs)
- Increased fluid output
- Urinary frequency
- Weight extremes

Readiness for Enhanced Fluid Balance

DEFINITION

Pattern of equilibrium between fluid volume and chemical composition of body fluids that is sufficient for meeting physical needs and can be strengthened

DEFINING CHARACTERISTICS

- Expresses desire/willingness to enhance fluid balance
- Stable weight
- Fluid intake meets daily need; no excessive thirst
- Straw-colored urine
- Specific gravity within normal limits
- Moist mucous membranes
- Good tissue turgor
- Urine output appropriate for intake
- No evidence of edema or dehydration

Impaired Skin Integrity*

DEFINITION

Break in dermis and/or epidermis (see also Pressure Ulcer)

DEFINING CHARACTERISTICS

Diagnostic Cues

- Disruption of skin surface (epidermis)
- Destruction of skin layers (dermis)
- Invasion of body structures (deep ulceration)

ETIOLOGICAL OR RELATED FACTORS

- Altered circulation, metabolic state
- Hyperthermia or hypothermia
- Humidity
- Alteration in turgor (elasticity)
- Altered nutritional status (obesity, emaciation)
- Altered pigmentation
- Developmental factors; psychogenic factors

HIGH-RISK POPULATIONS

- Physical immobilization
- Sensory-motor loss (cerebrovascular accident, spinal cord injury)
- Loss of consciousness
- Obesity
- Emaciation
- Immunological deficit
- Radiation

*See also Pressure Ulcer, Stage II–IV.

Risk for Impaired Skin Integrity or *Risk for Skin Breakdown**

DEFINITION

Presence of risk factors for skin ulceration/excoriation; use a risk assessment tool (e.g., Braden Scale) to determine risk

RISK FACTORS

- Unable to shift position at least every 1.5 to 2 hours (impaired mobility; immobilization)
- Reddened skin area (altered tissue perfusion), especially over bony prominences
- Verbalized pain or discomfort in local area, especially over bony prominences (possible deep-tissue damage)
- Presence of shearing forces, pressure (restraints, sustained pressure from casts), friction
- Nutritional deficit (e.g., protein, ascorbic acid deficiency)
- Excretions/secretions on skin
- Skeletal prominence
- Altered skin turgor (change in elasticity)
- Altered sensation, cognitive impairment (e.g., decreased consciousness)
- Altered metabolic state, anemia
- Altered circulation, edema, arteriosclerosis
- Psychogenic factors
- High humidity, environmental temperature
- Hypothermia or hyperthermia
- Medication (producing cellular breakdown)
- Altered pigmentation
- Decreased fatty tissue, skeletal prominence
- Immunologic factors
- Chemical substances on skin
- Radiation

*See also Pressure Ulcer, Stage I.

Impaired Tissue Integrity (Specify Type)

DEFINITION

Damage to mucous membrane or to corneal, integumentary, or subcutaneous tissue (specify type of tissue and impairment)

DEFINING CHARACTERISTICS

- Damaged or destroyed tissue (cornea, mucous membrane, integumentary, or subcutaneous)

ETIOLOGICAL OR RELATED FACTORS

- Altered circulation
- Nutritional deficit or excess
- Fluid deficit or excess
- Knowledge deficit
- Impaired physical mobility
- Irritants:
  - Chemical (body excretions, secretions, medications)
  - Thermal (temperature extremes)
  - Mechanical (pressure, shear, friction)
  - Radiation (including therapeutic radiation)

Pressure Ulcer (Specify Stage)*

DEFINITION

Break in skin integrity, usually over bony prominences, associated with lying or sitting for prolonged periods (specify stage)

DEFINING CHARACTERISTICS

Diagnostic Cues

+ Ulceration (disruption of skin surface, destruction of skin layers usually over bony prominences)

and/or

+ Verbalization of pain, discomfort, or numbness over bony prominence *without* exterior skin destruction (deep decubitus)

Stage I: Reddened area; no break in skin. (Note that reactive hyperemia can normally be expected to be present for 1–3 days as long as the pressure occludes blood flow to the area.)

Stage II: Reddened area; small ulceration. (Partial-thickness skin loss involving epidermis and/or dermis; the ulcer is superficial and appears clinically as an abrasion, blister, or shallow crater.)

Continues

*From Clinical Practice Guideline #3: *Pressure Ulcers in Adults: Prediction and Prevention.* Rockville, Md: USDHHS, Agency for Health Care Policy and Research; 1992. See this for detection, prevention, diagnosis, and treatment guidelines. Refer for medical evaluation if unresponsive to nursing measures and particularly if progression continues to Stage III or IV.

Pressure Ulcer (Specify Stage)—*cont'd*

Stage III: Deep ulceration with drainage; no necrosis. (Full-thickness skin loss involving damage to or necrosis of subcutaneous tissue that may extend down to, but not through, fascia; the ulcer appears clinically as a deep crater with or without undermining of adjacent tissue.)

Stage IV: Deep ulceration; necrotic area. (Full-thickness skin loss with extensive destruction; tissue necrosis or damage to muscle, bone, or supporting structures; and/or tendon or joint capsule; note that undermining and sinus tracts may also be associated with Stage IV pressure ulcers.)

ETIOLOGICAL OR RELATED FACTORS

- ◆ Prolonged pressure
- ◆ Friction, shear injury
- ◆ Immobility
- ◆ Incontinence
- ◆ Undernutrition (protein, vitamin C)
- ◆ Sensory-motor loss
- ◆ Cognitive impairment

HIGH-RISK POPULATIONS

- ◆ Hemiplegia, quadriplegia, hemiparesis (e.g., CVA, spinal cord injury)
- ◆ Orthopedic problems with immobilization (e.g., femoral fracture)
- ◆ Bed rest (e.g., critical care)

Latex Allergy Response

DEFINITION

Allergic response to natural latex rubber products

DEFINING CHARACTERISTICS

Type I Reaction

- Immediate reactions (< 1 hour) to latex proteins (can be life threatening)
- Contact urticaria progressing to generalized symptoms
- Edema of the lips, tongue, uvula, and/or throat
- Shortness of breath, tightness in chest, wheezing, bronchospasm leading to respiratory arrest
- Hypotension, syncope, cardiac arrest
- Facial itching
- Oral itching
- Gastrointestinal characteristics
  - Abdominal pain
  - Nausea
- Generalized characteristics
  - Flushing
  - General discomfort
  - Generalized edema
  - Increasing complaint of total body warmth
  - Restlessness

May also include:

- Orofacial characteristics:
  - Edema of sclera or eyelids
  - Erythema and/or itching of the eyes
  - Tearing of the eyes
  - Nasal congestion, itching, and/or erythema
  - Rhinorrhea

Continues

Latex Allergy Response—*cont'd*

- ◆ Facial erythema
- ◆ Facial, oral itching
- ◆ Abdominal pain, nausea
- ◆ Generalized symptoms:
  - ◆ Flushing; increasing complaint of total body warmth
  - ◆ Generalized discomfort, generalized edema
  - ◆ Restless

Type IV Reaction

- ◆ Eczema
- ◆ Irritation, redness, chapped or cracked skin or blisters
- ◆ Reaction to additives causes discomfort (e.g., thiurams, carbamates)
- ◆ Delayed onset (hours)
- ◆ No immune mechanism response

Risk for Latex Allergy Response

DEFINITION

Risk for allergic response to natural latex rubber products

RISK FACTORS

- Multiple surgical procedures especially from infancy (e.g., spina bifida)
- Allergy to bananas, avocados, tropical fruits, kiwi, chestnuts
- Professions with daily exposure to latex (e.g., medicine, nursing, dentistry)
- Conditions needing continuous or intermittent catheterization
- History of reactions to latex (balloons, condoms, gloves)
- Allergies to poinsettia plants
- History of allergies and asthma

Ineffective Thermoregulation

DEFINITION

Temperature fluctuation between hypothermia and hyperthermia

DEFINING CHARACTERISTICS

Diagnostic Cues

- Fluctuations in body temperature above or below the normal range (see defining characteristics of Hypothermia and Hyperthermia)

ETIOLOGICAL OR RELATED FACTORS

- Fluctuating environmental temperature

HIGH-RISK POPULATIONS

- Trauma or illness influencing central regulation
- Extremes of age (prematurity, immaturity, very old)

Hyperthermia

DEFINITION

Body temperature elevated above normal range

DEFINING CHARACTERISTICS

Diagnostic Cues

- Increase in body temperature above normal range for age

Supporting Cues

- Flushed skin
- Skin warm to touch
- Increased respiratory rate
- Tachycardia
- Seizures or convulsions (a consequence of hyperthermia)

ETIOLOGICAL OR RELATED FACTORS

- Exposure to hot environment
- Vigorous activity
- Medications/anesthesia
- Inappropriate clothing
- Increased metabolic rate
- Illness or trauma
- Dehydration
- Inability or decreased ability to perspire

Hypothermia

DEFINITION

Body temperature reduced below normal range

DEFINING CHARACTERISTICS

Diagnostic Cues

+ Reduction in body temperature below normal range for age

Supporting Cues

+ Shivering (mild)
+ Cool skin; pallor (moderate); piloerection
+ Slow capillary refill
+ Tachycardia; cyanotic nail beds
+ Hypertension

ETIOLOGICAL OR RELATED FACTORS

+ Exposure to cool or cold environment
+ Illness or trauma
+ Inability or decreased ability to shiver
+ Malnutrition, decreased metabolic rate, inactivity, aging
+ Vasodilation, evaporation from skin in cool environment
+ Damage to hypothalamus

Risk for Imbalanced Body Temperature*

DEFINITION

Presence of risk factors for failure to maintain body temperature within normal range

RISK FACTORS

- Illness or trauma affecting temperature regulation
- Altered metabolic rate
- Dehydration
- Extremes of age
- Sedatives, anesthesia
- Medications causing vasoconstriction or vasodilation
- Exposure to cold/cool or warm/hot environments
- Inactivity or vigorous activity
- Inappropriate clothing for environmental temperature
- Extremes of weight

*See also Ineffective Thermoregulation.

NOTES

NOTES

NOTES

Elimination Pattern

Constipation

DEFINITION

Decrease in frequency of defecation accompanied by difficult or incomplete passage of hard, dry stool

DEFINING CHARACTERISTICS

Diagnostic Cues

- Bowel pattern: decreased frequency or volume
- Dry, hard, formed stool or unable to pass stool
- Reports feeling of rectal fullness or pressure

Supporting Cues

- Straining with defecation
- Pain with defecation
- Abdominal tenderness with or without palpable muscle resistance; abdominal pain
- Distended abdomen; palpable rectal mass; palpable abdominal mass
- Increased abdominal pressure
- Abdominal dullness on percussion; borborygmi; hyperactive or hypoactive bowel sounds
- Severe flatus
- Presence of soft pastelike stool in rectum
- Anorexia, headache, indigestion; generalized fatigue
- Nausea, vomiting
- Bright red blood with stool
- Black or tarry stool

Older Adults (additional)

- Change in mental status
- Urinary incontinence
- Unexplained falls
- Elevated body temperature

ETIOLOGICAL OR RELATED FACTORS
Functional

- Habitual denial/ignoring of urge to defecate
- Inadequate toileting (timeliness, positioning for defecation, privacy; irregular defecation habits)
- Insufficient physical activity
- Abdominal muscle weakness

Psychological

- Depression
- Emotional stress
- Mental confusion

Mechanical

- Obesity
- Hemorrhoids

HIGH-RISK POPULATIONS
Pharmacological

- Laxative overdose
- Antilipemic agents
- Calcium carbonate; aluminum-containing antacids
- Nonsteroid anti-inflammatory agents
- Opiates, sedatives, antidepressants, phenothiazides
- Anticholinergics, bismuth salts
- Diuretics, sympathomimetics, calcium channel blockers

Mechanical

- Rectal abscess or ulcer, anal fissures, tumors, anal stricture
- Pregnancy
- Megacolon (Hirschsprung's disease)

Continues

Constipation—*cont'd*

- Electrolyteimbalance
- Rectal prolapse
- Prostate enlargement
- Neurological impairment
- Rectocele
- Postsurgical obstruction

Perceived Constipation

DEFINITION

Self-diagnosis of constipation and ensures daily bowel movement through abuse of laxatives, enemas, and/or suppositories

DEFINING CHARACTERISTICS

Diagnostic Cues

- ◆ Expectation of a daily bowel movement resulting in overuse of laxatives, enemas, and/or suppositories
- ◆ Expected passage of stool at same time every day

ETIOLOGICAL OR RELATED FACTORS

- ◆ Cultural or family health beliefs
- ◆ Faulty appraisal
- ◆ Impaired thought processes

Intermittent Constipation Pattern

DEFINITION

Periodic episodes of hard, dry stools or absence of stools not associated with a pathological state

DEFINING CHARACTERISTICS

Diagnostic Cues

- Reported or observed episodes of hard, dry stools or absence of stools occurring two to three times per month or more frequently
- Straining at stool

Supporting Cues

- Painful defecation
- Reported feeling of abdominal or rectal fullness; abdominal distention; back pain
- Reported feeling of pressure in rectum
- Use of laxatives
- Headache
- Appetite impairment
- Abdominal pain, cramps
- Palpable mass
- Nausea

ETIOLOGICAL OR RELATED FACTORS

- Low-roughage diet
- Low fluid intake
- Absence of routines (time)
- Decreased activity level
- Routine use of enemas, laxatives

HIGH-RISK POPULATIONS

- Hemorrhoids
- Antacids
- Therapeutic bed rest

Risk for Constipation

DEFINITION

Presence of risk factors for a decrease in frequency of defecation and difficult or incomplete passage of stool and/or passage of excessively hard, dry stool

RISK FACTORS

Dietary Factors

+ Dehydration, insufficient fiber intake, poor eating habits, change in usual foods and eating patterns
+ Decreased motility of GI tract
+ Inadequate dentition or oral hygiene
+ Insufficient fluid intake

Functional Factors

+ Insufficient physical activity
+ Irregular defecation habits (e.g., timeliness)
+ Change in usual positioning for defecation
+ Loss of privacy
+ Abdominal muscle weakness
+ Habitual denial or ignoring of urge to defecate
+ Recent environmental change influencing habit pattern

Psychological Factors

+ Depression
+ Emotional stress
+ Mental confusion

Pharmacological Factors

+ Aluminum-containing antacids
+ Anticholinergics

Continues

137

Risk for Constipation—*cont'd*

- Anticonvulsants
- Antidepressants
- Antilipemic agents
- Bismuth salts, calcium carbonate
- Calcium channel blockers
- Diuretics, laxative overuse
- Nonsteroidal anti-inflammatory agents
- Opiates, sedatives
- Phenothiazides, sympathomimetics

Mechanical Factors

- Obesity, pregnancy, postsurgical obstruction
- Prostate enlargement
- Rectal prolapse, rectocele
- Rectal or anal stricture, fissure, prolapse, abscess
- Cerebral vascular accident
- Electrolyte imbalance
- Hemorrhoids, megacolon (Hirschsprung's disease)

Diarrhea

DEFINITION

Passage of loose, unformed stools

DEFINING CHARACTERISTICS

Diagnostic Cues

- At least three liquid, loose stools per day

Supporting Cues

- Hyperactive bowel sounds
- Urgency
- Abdominal pain
- Cramping

ETIOLOGICAL OR RELATED FACTORS

- Laxative abuse
- Tube feedings
- Travel (bacteria, etc., in food and water)
- Alcohol abuse
- High stress or anxiety

HIGH-RISK POPULATIONS

- Infectious processes (parasites, toxins)
- Medications
- Inflammation, irritation
- Contaminants
- Radiation
- Malabsorption

Bowel Incontinence

DEFINITION

Change in bowel habits characterized by involuntary passage of stool

DEFINING CHARACTERISTICS

Diagnostic Cues

+ Involuntary passage of stool

Supporting Cues

+ Reports inability to delay defecation
+ Inattention to urge to defecate
+ Inability to recognize urge to defecate
+ Reports inability to feel rectal fullness
+ Recognizes rectal fullness but reports inability to expel formed stool
+ Constant dribbling of soft stool
+ Fecal odor
+ Fecal staining of clothing or bedding
+ Red perianal skin
+ Urgency

RELATED FACTORS

+ Environmental factors (e.g., inaccessible bathroom)
+ Cognitive impairment
+ Abnormally high abdominal or intestinal pressure (from gas)
+ Laxative abuse; dietary habits
+ Immobility; general decline in muscle tone (e.g., abdominal, perineal, bowel sphincter)
+ Impaction
+ Incomplete emptying of bowel

HIGH-RISK POPULATIONS

- Chronic diarrhea
- Rectal sphincter abnormality
- Colorectal lesions
- Impaired reservoir (bowel) capacity
- Medications
- Upper/lower motor nerve damage

Impaired Urinary Elimination

DEFINITION

An involuntary loss of urine at somewhat predictable intervals when a specific bladder volume is reached

DEFINING CHARACTERISTICS

- Incontinence
- Urgency
- Nocturia
- Hesitancy
- Frequency
- Dysuria
- Retention

RELATED FACTORS

- Urinary tract infection
- Anatomical obstruction
- Multiple causality
- Sensory-motor impairment

Functional Incontinence*

DEFINITION

Inability of usually continent person to reach toilet in time to avoid unintentional loss of urine

DEFINING CHARACTERISTICS

- Reports loss of urine before reaching toilet (accidents)
- Senses need to void but amount of time required to reach toilet exceeds length of time between sensing urge and uncontrolled voiding (loss of urine before reaching toilet)
- May only be incontinent in early morning
- Able to completely empty bladder

ETIOLOGICAL OR RELATED FACTORS

- Neuromuscular limitations
- Impaired vision
- Impaired cognition
- Psychological factors
- Environmental factors
- Weakened supporting pelvic structures

*NANDA International uses the name *functional urinary incontinence*.

Reflex Incontinence*

DEFINITION

Involuntary loss of urine at somewhat predictable intervals when a specific bladder volume is reached

DEFINING CHARACTERISTICS

Diagnostic Cues

- Predictable pattern of involuntary loss of urine
- No sensation of urge to void; no sensation of bladder fullness or voiding
- Unable to cognitively inhibit or initiate voiding

Supporting Cues

- Sensation of urge to void without voluntary inhibition of bladder contraction
- Sensations associated with full bladder such as sweating, restlessness, and abdominal discomfort
- Incomplete emptying with lesion above sacral micturition center
- Complete emptying with lesion above pontine micturition center

ETIOLOGICAL OR RELATED FACTORS

- Knowledge deficit (bladder management)

HIGH-RISK POPULATIONS

- Neurological impairment above level of sacral micturition center or pontine micturition center (e.g., myelomeningocele)

---

*NANDA International uses the name *reflex urinary incontinence*.

Stress Incontinence*

DEFINITION

Involuntary loss of urine of less than 50 ml occurring with increased abdominal pressure

DEFINING CHARACTERISTICS

Diagnostic Cues

- Reported or observed dribbling with increased abdominal pressure (sneezing, coughing, rising from low chair, laughing)

Supporting Cues

- Report of urinary urgency
- Urinary frequency (more often than every 2 hours)

ETIOLOGICAL OR RELATED FACTORS

- Weak pelvic muscles and structural supports
- Overdistention between voidings
- High intra-abdominal pressure (e.g., obesity)

HIGH-RISK POPULATIONS

- High intra-abdominal pressure (e.g., gravid uterus)
- Incompetent bladder outlet
- Age-related degenerative changes in pelvic muscles/structural supports
- Weak pelvic muscles and structural supports

*NANDA International uses the name *stress urinary incontinence*.

Urge Incontinence*

DEFINITION

Involuntary passage of urine occurring soon after a strong sense of urgency to void

DEFINING CHARACTERISTICS

Diagnostic Cues

- Inability to reach toilet in time with loss of urine
- Cannot hold or suppress urination urge (urinary urgency)

Supporting Cues

- Frequency (voiding more often than every 2 hours)
- Bladder contracture or spasm
- Nocturia (more than two times per night)
- Voiding in small amounts (less than 10 ml) or in large amounts (more than 550 ml)

ETIOLOGICAL OR RELATED FACTORS

- Alcohol, caffeine
- Increased fluid intake
- Increased urine concentration
- Overdistention of bladder

HIGH-RISK POPULATIONS

- Bladder spasm (irritation of bladder stretch receptors, e.g., bladder infection)
- Decreased bladder capacity (e.g., history of pelvic inflammatory disease, abdominal surgeries, indwelling urinary catheter)

---

*NANDA International uses the name *urge urinary incontinence*.

Risk for Urge Incontinence*

DEFINITION

Risk for involuntary loss of urine associated with a sudden, strong sensation of urgency

RISK FACTORS

- Ineffective toileting habits
- Effects of medications (caffeine, alcohol)
- Detrusor hyperreflexia from cystitis
- Detrusor muscle instability with impaired contractility
- Involuntary sphincter relaxation
- Small bladder capacity
- Urethritis
- Tumors, renal calculi
- Central nervous system disorders above pontine micturition center

*NANDA International uses the name *risk for urge urinary incontinence*.

Total Urinary Incontinence

DEFINITION

Continuous and unpredictable loss of urine

DEFINING CHARACTERISTICS

Diagnostic Cues

- Constant flow of urine at unpredictable times without distention or uninhibited bladder contractions or spasms
- Lack of perineal or bladder-filling awareness
- Unawareness of incontinence

Supporting Cues

- Nocturia
- Unsuccessful incontinence refractory treatments

ETIOLOGICAL OR RELATED FACTORS

- Ineffective incontinence management

HIGH-RISK POPULATIONS

- Neuropathy, e.g., trauma (spinal cord nerves preventing transmission of reflex indicating bladder fullness)
- Neurological dysfunction (triggering micturition at unpredictable times)
- Independent contraction of detrusor reflex (resulting from surgery)

Urinary Retention*

DEFINITION

Incomplete emptying of the bladder

DEFINING CHARACTERISTICS

Diagnostic Cues

- ◆ Bladder distention
- ◆ Small, frequent voiding or absence of urine output
- ◆ Residual urine in bladder (100 ml or more)

Supporting Cues

- ◆ Overflow incontinence
- ◆ Reports sensation of bladder fullness
- ◆ Dribbling
- ◆ Dysuria

ETIOLOGICAL OR RELATED FACTORS

- ◆ High urethral pressure (caused by weak detrusor)
- ◆ Blockage of urine

HIGH-RISK POPULATIONS

- ◆ Inhibition of reflex arc
- ◆ Strong sphincter

*If diagnosed, refer for medical evaluation unless attributable to not taking time
to empty bladder when voiding.

Readiness for Enhanced Urinary Elimination

DEFINITION

Pattern of urinary functions that is sufficient for meeting eliminatory needs and can be strengthened

DEFINING CHARACTERISTICS

- Expresses willingness to enhance urinary elimination
- Urine is straw colored with no odor
- Specific gravity within normal limits
- Amount of output within normal limits for age/other factors
- Positions self for emptying bladder
- Fluid intake adequate for daily needs

NOTES

NOTES

NOTES

NOTES

Activity-Exercise

Pattern

Activity Intolerance (Specify Level)

DEFINITION

Abnormal responses to energy-consuming body movements involved in required or desired daily activities

DEFINING CHARACTERISTICS

Diagnostic Cues*

- Report of dyspnea or shortness of breath or observation of difficulty breathing with activity
- Report of fatigue (evaluate in context of other cues)
- Heart rate changes (especially with cardiorespiratory problems)
- Muscle weakness, discomfort, pain (especially with neuromusculoskeletal problems)

and/or following energy-consuming activity:

- Failure of heart rate to return to normal (baseline rate) within approximately 3 minutes

Requiring Immediate Attention and Evaluation

- Reports discomfort or chest pain with activity (specify level of activity)
- Arrhythmias with activity (specify level of activity)
- Diastolic pressure increased by 15 mm Hg or more during activity
- Ischemic changes on ECG with activity (specify level of activity)
- Failure of blood pressure to increase with activity
- Dyspnea at rest (unless this is a baseline)

*Although there are a number of studies in nursing, the findings are not consistent on some indicators. Caution should be exercised and the activity stopped if intolerance is suspected.

ACTIVITY-EXERCISE PATTERN

Level I: Walk, regular pace, on level ground indefinitely; one flight or more but more short of breath than normally

Level II: Walk one city block 500 feet on level ground; climb one flight slowly without stopping

Level III: Walk no more than 50 feet on level ground without stopping; unable to climb one flight of stairs without stopping

Level IV: Dyspnea and fatigue at rest

ETIOLOGICAL OR RELATED FACTORS

+ Generalized weakness
+ Sedentary lifestyle

HIGH-RISK POPULATIONS

+ Imbalance between oxygen supply and demand (e.g., cardiovascular, pulmonary conditions, and changes with aging)
+ Activity progression (e.g., cardiac and other rehabilitation)
+ Long term bed rest or immobility, deconditioned status

Risk for Activity Intolerance

DEFINITION

Presence of risk factors for abnormal response to energy-consuming body movements

RISK FACTORS

- Deconditioned status (prolonged bed rest, inactivity)
- Documented respiratory problems
- Documented cardiac problems
- History of previous intolerance to activity
- Documented circulatory problems
- Currently on an activity-progression program
- Desire or need to engage in a higher level of activity
- Inexperience with the activity
- Generalized weakness (chronic disease)

Sedentary Lifestyle

DEFINITION

Reports a habit of life that is characterized by a low physical activity level

DEFINING CHARACTERISTICS

- Chooses a daily routine lacking physical exercise
- Demonstrates physical deconditioning
- Verbalizes preference for activities low in physical activity

ETIOLOGICAL OR RELATED FACTORS

- Knowledge deficit (health benefits of exercise)
- Lack of training for accomplishment of physical exercise
- Lack of resources (time, money, companionship, facilities)
- Lack of motivation/interest

Fatigue

DEFINITION

Overwhelming, sustained sense of exhaustion and decreased capacity for physical and mental work at usual level

DEFINING CHARACTERISTICS

Diagnostic Cues

+ Reports unremitting and overwhelming lack of energy
+ Insufficient energy to maintain usual routine (physical activity, required tasks; decreased work performance)

Supporting Cues

+ Increase in rest requirements; inability to restore energy even after sleep
+ Drowsy, tired, listless
+ Irritable
+ Increase in physical complaints
+ Decreased concentration
+ Compromised libido
+ Disinterest in surroundings
+ Feelings of guilt for not keeping up with responsibilities

ETIOLOGICAL AND RELATED FACTORS

Physiological Factors

+ Sleep deprivation
+ Poor physical condition
+ Malnutrition
+ Increased physical exertion

ACTIVITY-EXERCISE PATTERN

Psychological Factors

- Stress
- Anxiety
- Depression
- Boring lifestyle

Situational Factors

- Negative life events
- Occupation

Environmental Factors

- Lights, noise during sleep time
- Humidity
- Temperature

HIGH-RISK POPULATIONS

- Anemia
- Disease states
- Pregnancy

Deficient Diversional Activity

DEFINITION

Decreased engagement in recreational or leisure activities

DEFINING CHARACTERISTICS

Diagnostic Cues

- Expressed wish for something to do, such as read
- Report of boredom or daytime napping

Supporting Cues

- States usual hobbies or activities cannot be undertaken (e.g., in hospital)

ETIOLOGICAL OR RELATED FACTORS

- Long-term hospitalization apathy
- Environmental lack of diversional activity

HIGH-RISK POPULATIONS

- Frequent lengthy treatments
- Long-term illness
- High job and/or family demands

Impaired Physical Mobility (Specify Level)

DEFINITION

Limitation of independent, purposeful body movement in the environment

DEFINING CHARACTERISTICS

Diagnostic Cues

+ Inability to purposefully move within the physical environment
+ Postural instability during performance of routine activities
+ Decreased muscle control, strength, or mass

Supporting Cues

+ Gait changes (e.g., decreased walk speed, difficulty initiating gait, small steps, shuffles feet, exaggerated lateral postural sway)
+ Reluctance to initiate movement (e.g., fear, insufficient self-efficacy)
+ Engages in substitutions for movement (e.g., fixation on activity, increased attention to other's activity, controlling behavior, focus on preillness or predisability activity)

Functional Level Classification

Level I: Requires use of equipment or device
Level II: Requires help from another person for assistance, supervision, or teaching
Level III: Requires help from another person and equipment or device
Level IV: Dependent; does not participate in activity

Continues

Impaired Physical Mobility (Specify Level)—*cont'd*

ETIOLOGICAL OR RELATED FACTORS

- Activity intolerance (e.g., movement-induced shortness of breath, limited cardiovascular endurance)
- Joint stiffness or contractures (limited range of motion)
- Pain, discomfort
- Musculoskeletal impairment (e.g., loss of integrity of bone structures)
- Neuromuscular impairment (e.g., limited ability to perform fine/gross motor skills, uncoordinated or jerky movements, movement-induced tremor)
- Cognitive–sensory-perceptual impairment (e.g., decreased reaction time)
- Depressive mood state or anxiety
- Sedentary lifestyle, disuse, deconditioning
- Body mass index above 75th age-appropriate percentile
- Prescribed movement restriction (e.g., physical or chemical restraints, bed rest prescription, use of mechanical equipment that restricts movement, therapeutic immobilization)

Impaired Walking (Specify Level)

DEFINITION

Limitation of independent movement within the environment on foot (or with a device, e.g., cane, crutches, walker)

DEFINING CHARACTERISTICS

Diagnostic Cues

One or more of the following:
+ Impaired ability to climb stairs
+ Impaired ability to walk required distances
+ Impaired ability to walk on an incline or decline
+ Impaired ability to walk on uneven surfaces
+ Impaired ability to navigate curbs

Functional Level Classification

Level I: Requires use of equipment or device (cane, crutches, walker)

Level II: Requires help from another person(s) for assistance, supervision, teaching

Level III: Requires help from another person(s) and equipment or device

Level IV: Dependent; does not participate in movement

ETIOLOGICAL OR RELATED FACTORS

+ None

HIGH-RISK POPULATIONS

+ Marked obesity
+ Sensory-motor loss
+ Severe arthritis
+ Severe weakness

Impaired Wheelchair Mobility

DEFINITION

Limitation of independent operation of wheelchair within the environment

DEFINING CHARACTERISTICS

Diagnostic Cues

One or more of the following:

- Impaired ability to operate manual or power wheelchair on even or uneven surface
- Impaired ability to operate manual or power wheelchair on an incline or decline
- Impaired ability to operate wheelchair on curbs

ETIOLOGICAL OR RELATED FACTORS

- None

HIGH-RISK POPULATIONS

- Sensory or neuromuscular loss (e.g., spinal cord injury, muscular dystrophy, cerebral vascular accident)
- Marked weakness
- Severe arthritis

ACTIVITY-EXERCISE PATTERN

Impaired Bed Mobility (Specify Level)

DEFINITION

Limitation of independent movement from one bed position to another

DEFINING CHARACTERISTICS

Diagnostic Cues

One or more of the following:
- Impaired ability to turn side to side
- Impaired ability to move from supine to sitting or sitting to supine
- Impaired ability to "scoot" or reposition self in bed
- Impaired ability to move from supine to prone or prone to supine
- Impaired ability to move from supine to long sitting or long sitting to supine

Functional Level Classification

Level I: Requires use of equipment or device
Level II: Requires help from another person(s) for assistance, supervision, teaching
Level III: Requires help from another person(s) and equipment or device
Level IV: Dependent; does not participate in movement

ETIOLOGICAL OR RELATED FACTORS

- None

HIGH-RISK POPULATIONS

- Paralysis
- Coma
- Marked weakness
- Marked obesity

Impaired Transfer Ability (Specify Level)

DEFINITION

Limitation of independent body movement between two nearby surfaces

DEFINING CHARACTERISTICS

Diagnostic Cues

One or more of the following:

- Impaired ability to transfer from bed to chair and chair to bed
- Impaired ability to transfer on or off a toilet or commode
- Impaired ability to transfer in and out of tub or shower
- Impaired ability to transfer between uneven levels
- Impaired ability to transfer from chair to car or car to chair
- Impaired ability to transfer from chair to floor or floor to chair
- Impaired ability to transfer from standing to floor or floor to standing

Functional Level Classification

Level I: Requires use of equipment or device

Level II: Requires help from another person(s) for assistance, supervision, teaching

Level III: Requires help from another person(s) and equipment or device

Level IV: Dependent; does not participate in movement

ETIOLOGICAL OR RELATED FACTORS

- None

HIGH-RISK POPULATIONS

- Paralysis
- Peripheral sensory loss
- Marked weakness
- Marked obesity
- Limb amputation

Wandering

DEFINITION

Meandering, aimless, or repetitive locomotion that exposes the individual to harm; frequently incongruent with boundaries, limits, or obstacles; may be sporadic or continual

DEFINING CHARACTERISTICS

- Frequent or continuous movement from place to place, often revisiting the same destinations
- Persistent locomotion in search of "missing" or unattainable people
- Haphazard locomotion
- Locomotion into unauthorized or private spaces
- Locomotion resulting in unintended leaving of premises
- Long periods of locomotion without an apparent destination
- Fretful locomotion or pacing
- Inability to locate significant landmarks in a familiar setting
- Locomotion that cannot be easily dissuaded or redirected
- Following behind or shadowing a caregiver's locomotion
- Trespassing
- Hyperactivity
- Scanning, seeking, or searching behaviors
- Periods of locomotion interspersed with periods of nonlocomotion (e.g., sitting, standing, sleeping)
- Multiple episodes of getting lost

ETIOLOGICAL OR RELATED FACTORS

- Cognitive impairment, specifically memory and recall deficits, disorientation, poor visuoconstructive (or visuospatial) ability, language defects (primarily expressive)
- Cortical atrophy
- Premorbid behavior (e.g., outgoing, sociable personality; premorbid dementia)
- Separation from familiar people and places
- Sedation
- Frustration, anxiety, boredom, depression (agitation)
- Over/understimulating social or physical environment
- Physiological state or need (e.g., hunger/thirst, pain, urination, constipation)
- Time of day

Risk for Disuse Syndrome*

DEFINITION

Presence of risk factors for deterioration of body systems as the result of prescribed or unavoidable musculoskeletal inactivity

RISK FACTORS

- Paralysis
- Mechanical immobilization (e.g., lower-body cast, leg traction, vascular lines)
- Prescribed immobilization
- Severe pain
- Altered level of consciousness
- Severe depression

---

*Complications of immobility can include pressure ulcer, constipation, stasis of pulmonary secretions, thrombosis, urinary tract infection and/or retention, decreased strength or endurance, orthostatic hypotension, decreased range of joint motion, disorientation, body image disturbance, and powerlessness.

Risk for Joint Contractures

DEFINITION

Presence of risk factors for shortening of tendons at movable joints (back, head, upper and lower extremities)

RISK FACTORS

- Loss of voluntary postural muscle control
- Prolonged joint flexion in sitting or recumbent position
- Spasticity
- Report of pain or discomfort on movement
- Imposed restrictions of joint movement (e.g., casts, traction)
- Assumption of abnormal posture resulting from psychosocial factors or cognitive deficit

Total Self Care Deficit (Specify Level)

DEFINITION

Inability to complete feeding, bathing, toileting, dressing, and grooming of self

DEFINING CHARACTERISTICS

Diagnostic Cues

+ Observation or valid report of inability to eat, bathe, toilet, dress, and groom self independently (see defining characteristics for each deficit on pp. 175–180)

Functional Level Classification

Level I: Requires use of equipment or devices
Level II: Requires help from another person(s) for assistance, supervision, teaching
Level III: Requires help from another person(s) and equipment or device
Level IV: Dependent; does not participate in self care

ETIOLOGICAL OR RELATED FACTORS

+ Decreased activity tolerance, strength, and/or endurance
+ Pain or discomfort
+ Uncompensated perceptual-cognitive impairment (specify)
+ Uncompensated neuromuscular impairment (specify)
+ Uncompensated musculoskeletal impairment (specify)
+ Severe anxiety
+ Depression
+ Environmental barriers

Bathing-Hygiene Self Care Deficit (Specify Level)

DEFINITION

Impaired ability to perform or complete bathing and hygiene activities

DEFINING CHARACTERISTICS

Diagnostic Cues

+ Impaired ability to wash body or body parts

and one or more of the following:

+ Impaired ability to obtain water
+ Impaired ability to get to water source (tub, shower, sink)
+ Impaired ability to regulate water temperature or flow

Functional Level Classification

Level I: Requires use of equipment or devices
Level II: Requires help from another person(s) for assistance, supervision, teaching
Level III: Requires help from another person(s) and equipment or device
Level IV: Dependent; does not participate in self care bathing or hygiene

ETIOLOGICAL OR RELATED FACTORS

+ Decreased activity tolerance, strength, and/or endurance
+ Pain or discomfort
+ Uncompensated perceptual-cognitive impairment (specify)
+ Uncompensated neuromuscular impairment (specify)
+ Uncompensated musculoskeletal impairment (specify)
+ Severe anxiety
+ Depression
+ Environmental barriers

Dressing-Grooming Self Care Deficit (Specify Level)

DEFINITION

Impaired ability to perform or complete dressing and grooming activities

DEFINING CHARACTERISTICS

Diagnostic Cues

- ♦ Inability to:
    - ♦ Choose clothing
    - ♦ Pick up clothing
    - ♦ Put on and take off necessary items of clothing on upper body
    - ♦ Put on and take off necessary items of clothing on lower body (put on socks and shoes)
    - ♦ Fasten clothing and use zippers

Supporting Cues

- ♦ Obtain or replace items of clothing (situation dependent)
- ♦ Maintain appearance at a satisfactory level

Functional Level Classification

Level I: Requires use of equipment or device
Level II: Requires help from another person for assistance, supervision, or teaching
Level III: Requires help from another person and equipment or device
Level IV: Dependent; does not participate in self-dressing or grooming

ACTIVITY-EXERCISE PATTERN

ETIOLOGICAL OR RELATED FACTORS

- Decreased activity tolerance, strength, and or endurance (weakness or tiredness)
- Pain, discomfort
- Uncompensated perceptual or cognitive impairment
- Uncompensated neuromuscular impairment
- Uncompensated musculoskeletal impairment
- Severe anxiety
- Environmental barriers
- Situational depression
- Decreased motivation or lack of motivation

Feeding Self Care Deficit (Specify Level)

DEFINITION

Impaired ability to perform or complete feeding activities

DEFINING CHARACTERISTICS

Diagnostic Cues

+ Inability to bring food from receptacle to the mouth

Supporting Cues

+ Inability to prepare food for ingestion
+ Inability to open containers
+ Inability to get food onto utensil and handle utensils
+ Inability to pick up cup or glass
+ Inability to complete a meal
+ Inability to ingest food in a socially acceptable manner
+ Inability to ingest food safely
+ Inability to ingest sufficient food

Functional Level Classification

Level I: Requires use of equipment or device
Level II: Requires help from another person for assistance, supervision, or teaching
Level III: Requires help from another person and equipment or device
Level IV: Dependent; does not participate in self-feeding

ETIOLOGICAL OR RELATED FACTORS

+ Decreased activity tolerance, strength, and/or endurance (weakness or tiredness)
+ Pain, discomfort
+ Uncompensated perceptual or cognitive impairment
+ Uncompensated neuromuscular impairment

ACTIVITY-EXERCISE PATTERN

+ Uncompensated musculoskeletal impairment
+ Severe anxiety
+ Environmental barriers
+ Situational depression
+ Decreased motivation or lack of motivation

Toileting Self Care Deficit (Specify Level)

DEFINITION

Impaired ability to perform or complete toileting activities

DEFINING CHARACTERISTICS

Diagnostic Cues

- Unable to get to toilet or commode
- Unable to carry out proper toilet hygiene
- Unable to manipulate clothing for toileting
- Unable to rise from toilet or commode

Supporting Cues

- Impaired ability to sit on toilet or commode
- Unable to flush toilet or empty commode

Functional Level Classification

Level I: Requires use of equipment or devices
Level II: Requires help from another person(s): assistance, supervision, teaching
Level III: Requires help from another person(s) and equipment or device
Level IV: Dependent; does not participate in self-toileting

ETIOLOGICAL OR RELATED FACTORS

- Transfer deficit
- Decreased activity tolerance, strength, and/or endurance
- Pain or discomfort
- Uncompensated perceptual-cognitive impairment (specify)
- Uncompensated neuromuscular impairment (specify)

ACTIVITY-EXERCISE PATTERN

- Uncompensated musculoskeletal impairment (specify)
- Severe anxiety
- Depression
- Environmental barriers

Developmental Delay: Self Care Skills (Specify Level)

DEFINITION

Demonstrates deviations from age-group norms for self care skills

DEFINING CHARACTERISTICS

Diagnostic Cues

- Delay or difficulty in performing self care skills typical of age-group or developmental level (eating, bathing, hygiene, toileting, dressing, grooming)

Supporting Cues

- Flat affect
- Listlessness
- Decreased responses

ETIOLOGICAL OR RELATED FACTORS

- Low-stimulation environment (social, physical)
- Environmental and stimulation deficiencies
- Inadequate caretaking
- Indifference
- Inconsistent responsiveness
- Multiple caretakers
- Separation (from significant others)
- Physical disability effects
- Prescribed dependence

Delayed Surgical Recovery

DEFINITION

Extension of the number of postoperative days required for individuals to initiate and perform activities that maintain life, health, and well-being

DEFINING CHARACTERISTICS

- Difficulty in moving about
- Requires help to complete self care
- Fatigue
- Report of pain or discomfort
- Postpones resumption of work or play (child)
- Reports perception that more time is needed to recover
- Evidence of interrupted healing of surgical area (e.g., red, indurated, draining, immobile)

ETIOLOGICAL OR RELATED FACTORS

(This diagnosis may be used to describe an etiological factor that is causing other problems.)

Delayed Growth and Development*

DEFINITION

Deviations in norms from his or her age group

DEFINING CHARACTERISTICS

- Delay or difficulty in performing skills (motor, social, or expressive) typical of age group
- Altered physical growth
- Inability to perform self care or self-control activities appropriate for age

ETIOLOGICAL OR RELATED FACTORS

- Inadequate caretaking
- Indifference
- Inconsistent responsiveness
- Multiple caretakers
- Separation (from significant others)
- Environmental and stimulation deficiencies
- Physical disability effects
- Prescribed dependence

*See Developmental Delay: Social Skills, Language Skills, Communication Skills.

Risk for Delayed Development*

DEFINITION

Risk for delay of 25% or more in one or more of the areas of social or self-regulatory behavior, or cognitive, language, gross, or fine motor skills

RISK FACTORS

Prenatal Factors

+ Maternal age younger than 15 or older than 35 years
+ Substance abuse
+ Genetic or endocrine disorders
+ Maternal inadequate nutrition
+ Late, poor, or lack of prenatal care
+ Illiteracy, poverty

Physiological Factors

+ Malnutrition, failure to thrive
+ Seizures
+ Positive drug screening test
+ Brain damage (e.g., hemorrhage in postnatal period, shaken baby, abuse, accident)
+ Vision or hearing impairment or frequent otitis media
+ Technology dependent
+ Lead poisoning
+ Prematurity
+ Chemotherapy, radiation therapy

*See Developmental Delay: Social Skills, Language Skills, Communication Skills.

Psychosocial Factors

- Deprivation
- Violence
- Behavior disorders
- Natural disaster
- Caregiver mental illness, retardation, severe learning disability
- Foster or adopted child

Risk for Disproportionate Growth

DEFINITION

Risk for growth above the 97th percentile or below the 3rd percentile for age, crossing two percentile channels (disproportionate growth)

RISK FACTORS

Prenatal Factors

♦ Congenital or genetic disorders
♦ Maternal nutrition
♦ Multiple gestation
♦ Teratogen exposure
♦ Maternal substance use or abuse

Physiological Factors

♦ Malnutrition
♦ Maladaptive feeding behaviors
♦ Anorexia
♦ Insatiable appetite
♦ Infection
♦ Chronic illness
♦ Lead poisoning
♦ Prematurity

Psychosocial Factors

♦ Deprivation
♦ Violence
♦ Natural disasters
♦ Caregiver abuse
♦ Caregiver mental illness, retardation, severe learning disability

Impaired Home Maintenance

DEFINITION

Inability to independently maintain a safe, growth-promoting immediate environment (specify mild, moderate, severe, potential, or chronic)

DEFINING CHARACTERISTICS

Diagnostic Cues

- Household members express difficulty in maintaining their home in a comfortable fashion
- Household members request assistance with home maintenance

and one or more of the following:

- Disorderly surroundings; repeated hygienic disorders, infestations, or infections
- Offensive odors; accumulation of dirt, food wastes, or hygienic wastes
- Inappropriate household temperature; unwashed or unavailable cooking equipment, clothes, or linen
- Overtaxed family members (e.g., exhausted, anxious)
- Lack of necessary equipment or aids
- Presence of vermin or rodents
- Household members describe outstanding debts or financial crises

ETIOLOGICAL OR RELATED FACTORS

- Individual or family member illness or injury
- Support system deficit
- Insufficient family organization or planning
- Insufficient finances, outstanding debts, financial crises
- Unfamiliarity with neighborhood resources
- Impaired cognitive or emotional functioning
- Knowledge deficit (specify area)
- Lack of role modeling

ACTIVITY-EXERCISE PATTERN

HIGH-RISK POPULATIONS

- ◆ Chronic debilitating illness with fatigue
- ◆ History of lack of role models for home management

Dysfunctional Ventilatory Weaning Response

DEFINITION

Inability to adjust to lowered levels of mechanical ventilator support, which interrupts and prolongs the weaning process (mild, moderate, severe)

DEFINING CHARACTERISTICS

Diagnostic Cues

Mild

- Responds to lowered levels of mechanical ventilator support with:
  - Restlessness
  - Slight increase in respiratory rate from baseline and

may report or observe one or more of the following:
- Expression of increased need for oxygen, breathing discomfort, fatigue, warmth
- Queries about possible machine malfunction
- Increased concentration on breathing

Moderate

- Responds to lowered levels of mechanical ventilator support with:
  - Slight increase from baseline blood pressure (< 20 mm Hg)
  - Slight increase from baseline heart rate (< 20 beats/minute)
  - Baseline increase in respiratory rate (< 5 breaths/minute)

and one or more of the following:
- Hypervigilance to activities
- Inability to respond to coaching
- Inability to cooperate
- Apprehension

- Diaphoresis
- Eye widening ("wide-eyed look")
- Decreased air entry on auscultation
- Color changes (pale, slight cyanosis)
- Slight respiratory accessory muscle use

Severe

Responds to lowered levels of mechanical ventilator support with:

- Agitation
- Deterioration in arterial blood gases from current baseline
- Increase from baseline blood pressure > 20 mm Hg
- Increase from baseline heart rate > 20 beats/minute
- Respiratory rate increases significantly from baseline

and one or more of the following:

- Profuse diaphoresis
- Full respiratory accessory muscle use
- Shallow, gasping breaths
- Paradoxical abdominal breathing
- Discoordinated breathing with the ventilator
- Decreased level of consciousness
- Adventitious breath sounds, audible airway secretions
- Cyanosis

Supporting Cues

- History of ventilator dependence > 1 week
- History of multiple unsuccessful weaning attempts

ETIOLOGICAL OR RELATED FACTORS

Physiological Factors

- Ineffective airway clearance
- Disturbed sleep pattern

Continues

Dysfunctional Ventilatory Weaning Response—*cont'd*

- ◆ Inadequate nutrition
- ◆ Uncontrolled pain or discomfort

Psychological Factors

- ◆ Knowledge deficit (weaning process, patient role)
- ◆ Perceived inability to wean
- ◆ Decreased motivation
- ◆ Decreased self-esteem
- ◆ Anxiety: moderate, severe
- ◆ Fear
- ◆ Hopelessness
- ◆ Powerlessness
- ◆ Insufficient trust in the nurse

Situational Factors

- ◆ Uncontrolled episodic energy demands or problems
- ◆ Inappropriate pacing of diminished ventilator support
- ◆ Inadequate social support
- ◆ Adverse environment (e.g., noisy, active environment; negative events in the room; low nurse/patient ratio; extended nurse absence from bedside; unfamiliar nursing staff)

HIGH-RISK POPULATIONS

- ◆ Prolonged ventilator dependency
- ◆ Severe chronic pulmonary disease

Impaired Spontaneous Ventilation*

DEFINITION

Decreased energy or reserves resulting in an individual's inability to maintain breathing adequate to support life

DEFINING CHARACTERISTICS

- Dyspnea
- Increased metabolic rate
- Increased restlessness
- Apprehension
- Increased use of accessory muscles
- Decreased tidal volume
- Increased heart rate
- Decreased pO_2
- Increased pCO_2
- Decreased SaO_2

ETIOLOGICAL OR RELATED FACTORS

- Metabolic factors (specify)
- Respiratory muscle fatigue

*If diagnosed, refer for immediate medical evaluation.

Ineffective Airway Clearance

DEFINITION

Inability to effectively clear secretions or obstruction from respiratory tract

DEFINING CHARACTERISTICS

Diagnostic Cues

- Adventitious breath sounds (specify location): crackles (rales), rhonchi, wheezes
- Unable to clear airways; cough ineffective or absent

Progressing to:

- Reports shortness of breath or difficulty breathing
- Requires frequent suctioning
- Respiratory rate increase (tachypnea) or depth changes
- Decreased breath sounds
- Hypoxemia

Supporting Cues

- Dyspnea at rest or on exertion
- Hypercapnia
- Cyanosis

ETIOLOGICAL OR RELATED FACTORS

- Ineffective cough
- Excess thick secretions
- Decreased energy or fatigue
- Pain (specify area)
- Presence of artificial airway

HIGH-RISK POPULATIONS

- Airway obstruction
- Tracheobronchial infection
- Trauma
- Perceptual or cognitive impairment

Ineffective Breathing Pattern

DEFINITION

Inspiration and/or expiration that does not provide adequate ventilation

DEFINING CHARACTERISTICS

Diagnostic Cues

- Reports shortness of breath/difficulty breathing
- Dyspnea at rest or on exertion
- Respiratory rate and/or depth changes
- Use of accessory muscles to breathe
- Respiratory rate/min
  - Infants: < 25 or > 60
  - Ages 1–4: < 20 or > 30
  - Ages 5–14: < 14 or > 25
  - Adults > 14 yrs: ≤ 11 or > 24
- Depth of breathing
  - Adult tidal volume: 500 ml at rest
  - Infant tidal volume: 6–8 ml/kg
- Timing ratio
- Decreased vital capacity
- Nasal flaring
- Reports feeling anxious or apprehensive
- Decreased inspiratory/expiratory pressure
- Decreased minute ventilation

Supporting Cues

- Pursed-lip breathing
- Reduced motion of chest, prolonged expiratory phase
- Cyanosis
- Orthopnea

Continues

Ineffective Breathing Pattern—*cont'd*

- Nasal flaring
- Abnormal arterial blood gases
- Fremitus
- Increased anteroposterior chest diameter
- Assumption of three-point position

ETIOLOGICAL OR RELATED FACTORS

- Anxiety
- Decreased energy or fatigue
- Pain
- Knowledge deficit (compensatory breathing patterns)
- Bone deformity
- Obesity
- Spinal cord injury
- Body position
- Respiratory muscle fatigue

HIGH-RISK POPULATIONS

- Neuromusculoskeletal impairment (e.g., spinal cord injury, bony deformity, neurological immaturity)
- Perceptual or cognitive impairment
- Respiratory muscle fatigue
- Chest wall deformity
- Hyperventilation
- Hypoventilation syndrome

Impaired Gas Exchange*

DEFINITION

Excess or deficit in oxygenation and/or carbon dioxide elimination at the alveolar-capillary level

DEFINING CHARACTERISTICS

- Reports shortness of breath or difficulty breathing
- Abnormal respiratory rate, rhythm, depth (specify)
- Dyspnea
- Hypoxemia
- Hypercapnia
- Abnormal blood gases, abnormal arterial pH
- Abnormal skin color (pale, dusky, cyanosis)
- Diaphoresis
- Visual disturbances
- Tachycardia
- Restlessness, anxiety
- Confusion, somnolence, irritability
- Headache when awakening

ETIOLOGICAL OR RELATED FACTORS

- Ventilation-perfusion imbalance
- Alveolar-capillary changes

*If diagnosed, refer for medical evaluation.

Decreased Cardiac Output*

DEFINITION

Inadequate blood pumped by the heart to meet the metabolic demands of the body

DEFINING CHARACTERISTICS

Altered Heart Rate/Rhythm

+ Arrhythmias (tachycardia, bradycardia)
+ Palpitations
+ EKG changes

Altered Preload

+ Jugular vein distention
+ Fatigue
+ Edema
+ Murmurs
+ Increased/decreased central venous pressure (CVP)
+ Increased/decreased pulmonary artery wedge pressure (PAWP)
+ Weight gain

Altered Afterload

+ Cold/clammy skin
+ Shortness of breath/dyspnea
+ Oliguria
+ Prolonged capillary refill
+ Decreased peripheral pulses
+ Variations in blood pressure readings
+ Increased/decreased systemic vascular resistance (SVR)
+ Increased/decreased pulmonary vascular resistance (PVR)
+ Skin color changes (pallor)

*If diagnosed, refer for medical evaluation.

ACTIVITY-EXERCISE PATTERN

Altered Contractility

- Crackles
- Cough
- Orthopnea/paroxysmal nocturnal dyspnea
- Cardiac output < 4 L/min
- Cardiac index < 2.5 L/min
- Decreased ejection fraction
- Stroke volume index (SVI)
- Left ventricular stroke work index (LVSWI)
- S_3 or S_4 sounds

Behavioral/Emotional

- Restlessness
- Anxiety

ETIOLOGICAL OR RELATED FACTORS

(Factors listed by NANDA International are same as defining characteristics.)

Ineffective Tissue Perfusion (Specify Type)*

DEFINITION

Decrease in blood supply (nutrition and oxygenation) resulting in the failure to nourish tissues at the capillary level (specify cerebral, cardiopulmonary, renal, gastrointestinal, and/or peripheral)

DEFINING CHARACTERISTICS

Peripheral

- Cold extremities
- Edema
- Extremities blue or purple when dependent; pale on elevation and color does not return on lowering leg
- Diminished arterial pulsations
- Shiny skin surfaces; lack of lanugo hair
- Round scars covered with atrophied skin
- Slow-growing, dry, thick, brittle nails
- Claudication
- Blood pressure changes in extremities
- Bruits
- Slow healing of lesions; gangrene

Renal

- Hematuria
- Oliguria or anuria
- Elevated BUN/creatinine ratio

Gastrointestinal

- Hypoactive or absent bowel sounds
- Nausea
- Abdominal distention
- Abdominal pain or tenderness

*If diagnosed, refer for medical evaluation.

ACTIVITY-EXERCISE PATTERN

Cerebral

- Speech abnormalities
- Pupillary changes
- Weakness or paralysis of extremities
- Altered mental status
- Difficulty swallowing

Cardiopulmonary

- Capillary refill > 3 seconds
- Abnormal arterial blood gases
- Chest pain, dyspnea
- Sense of "impending doom"
- Arrhythmias
- Nasal flaring
- Chest retraction
- Respiratory rate outside of acceptable parameters

ETIOLOGICAL OR RELATED FACTORS

- Interruption of arterial flow
- Interruption of venous flow
- Exchange problems
- Hypovolemia or hypervolemia

201

Autonomic Dysreflexia

DEFINITION

Life-threatening uninhibited sympathetic nervous system response to a noxious stimulus with a spinal cord injury of T7 or above

DEFINING CHARACTERISTICS

- Spinal cord injury (T7 or above)
- Paroxysmal hypertension (sudden, periodic elevated blood pressure; systolic pressure > 140 mm Hg and diastolic > 90 mm Hg)
- Diaphoresis (above the injury)
- Headache (a diffuse pain in different portions of the head; not confined to any nerve distribution area)
- Bradycardia or tachycardia (pulse rate of < 60 or > 100 beats per minute)
- Red splotches on skin (above the injury); pallor below the injury
- Chilling; pilomotor reflex (gooseflesh formation when skin is cooled)
- Paresthesia, blurred vision
- Conjunctival congestion, nasal congestion
- Horner's syndrome (contraction of the pupil, partial ptosis of the eyelid, enophthalmos, sometimes loss of sweating over the affected side of the face)
- Metallic taste in mouth
- Chest pain

ETIOLOGICAL OR RELATED FACTORS

- Bladder distention
- Bowel distention
- Skin irritation

Risk for Autonomic Dysreflexia

DEFINITION

Risk for life-threatening, uninhibited response of the sympathetic nervous system with spinal cord lesion at T6 or above (following spinal shock); has been demonstrated in patients with injuries at T7 or T8

RISK FACTORS

Injury or lesion at T6 and at least one of the following painful or irritating stimuli:

PHYSIOLOGICAL FACTORS

- Bladder distention, spasm
- Catheterization
- Epididymitis, urethritis, urinary tract infection
- Constipation, enemas, stimulation (digital, instrumentation)
- Painful or irritating stimuli below level of injury
- Gastrointestinal pathology (e.g., gastric ulcers, esophageal reflux)
- Bowel distention
- Constipation, fecal impaction
- Digital stimulation, enemas
- Suppositories
- Hemorrhoids
- Temperature fluctuations
- Menstruation, sexual intercourse, ejaculation
- Cutaneous stimuli (pressure ulcer, ingrown toenail, dressings, burns, rash, heterotrophic bone)

Continues

Risk for Autonomic Dysreflexia—*cont'd*

Situational Factors

+ Positioning, range-of-motion exercises, pregnancy, labor and delivery, drug reactions (decongestants, sympathomimetics, vasoconstrictors, narcotic withdrawal)
+ Constrictive clothing
+ Fractures
+ Deep vein thrombosis
+ Ovarian cyst
+ Surgical procedures

Risk for Sudden Infant Death Syndrome

DEFINITION

Presence of risk factors for sudden death of an infant

RISK FACTORS

Modifiable Factors

- Infants placed to sleep in the prone or side lying position
- Prenatal and/or postnatal infant smoke exposure
- Infant overheating/overwrapping
- Soft underlayment/loose articles in the sleep environment
- Delayed or no prenatal care

Potentially Modifiable Factors

- Low birth weight
- Prematurity
- Young maternal age

Nonmodifiable Factors

- Male gender
- Ethnicity (e.g., African-American or Native American race of mother)
- Seasonality of SIDS deaths (higher in winter and fall months)
- SIDS mortality peaks between infant age of 2–4 months

Disorganized Infant Behavior

DEFINITION

Disintegrated physiological and neurobehavioral responses to the environment

DEFINING CHARACTERISTICS

Physiological/Regulatory System

- Irritability
- Inability to inhibit autonomic system:
  - Heart rate (e.g., bradycardia, tachycardia, arrhythmias)
  - Respiratory rate (e.g., bradypnea, tachypnea, apnea)
  - Color (e.g., pale, cyanotic, mottled, flushed)
- Oximeter desaturation
- Feeding intolerance (e.g., aspiration or emesis)
- Time-out signals (e.g., gaze, grasp, hiccough, cough, sneeze, yawn, sigh, slack jaw, open mouth, tongue thrust)
- Malnutrition
- Feeding intolerance

Motor System

- Increased or decreased muscle tone; limpness
- Tremors, startles, twitches; jittery, jerky, uncoordinated movement
- Hyperextension of arms and legs, finger splay, fisting or hands to face, altered primitive reflexes

State-Organization System

- Sleep is diffuse or unclear, state oscillation
- Quiet-awake (staring, gaze aversion)
- Active-awake (fussy, worried gaze)
- Irritable or panicky crying

ACTIVITY-EXERCISE PATTERN

Attention-Interaction System

+ Abnormal response to sensory stimuli (e.g., difficult to soothe; inability to sustain alert state)

ETIOLOGICAL OR RELATED FACTORS

+ Pain
+ Oral or motor problems
+ Invasive or painful procedure
+ Caregiver factors:
  + Cue misreading
  + Knowledge deficit (cues)
+ Environmental stimulation

HIGH-RISK POPULATIONS

+ Prenatal: Congenital or genetic disorders, teratogenic exposure
+ Postnatal: Prematurity
+ Individual factors: Gestational age, postconceptual age
+ Immature neurological system, illness

Risk for Disorganized Infant Behavior

DEFINITION

Risk for disintegration of physiological and neurobehavioral responses to the environment

RISK FACTORS

- ◆ Pain
- ◆ Oral or motor problems
- ◆ Environmental overstimulation
- ◆ Lack of containment or boundaries
- ◆ Invasive or painful procedures

Readiness for Enhanced Organized Infant Behavior

DEFINITION

Pattern of modulation of the physiological and functional behavioral systems of an infant (i.e., autonomic, motor, state, organizational, self-regulatory, and attentional-interactional systems) that is satisfactory but that can be improved, resulting in higher levels of integration in response to environmental stimuli

DEFINING CHARACTERISTICS

- Stable physiological measures
- Definite sleep-wake states
- Use of some self-regulatory behaviors
- Response to visual or auditory stimuli

ETIOLOGICAL OR RELATED FACTORS

- Prematurity
- Pain

Risk for Peripheral Neurovascular Dysfunction*

DEFINITION

Presence of risk factors for disruption in circulation, sensation, or motion of an extremity

RISK FACTORS

- ◆ Immobilization
- ◆ Mechanical compression (e.g., tourniquet, cast or brace, dressing or restraint)
- ◆ Orthopedic surgery
- ◆ Trauma
- ◆ Burns
- ◆ Vascular obstruction
- ◆ Fractures

*Diagnosis encompasses three foci (nutrient supply to tissues, sensation, and motion); thus it can be viewed as a potentially dysfunctional nutritional-metabolic, perceptual, or activity pattern.

Decreased Intracranial Adaptive Capacity

DEFINITION

Repeated disproportionate increases in intracranial pressure in response to noxious and nonnoxious stimuli due to lack of compensation for increases in intracranial volumes by intracranial fluid dynamic mechanisms

DEFINING CHARACTERISTICS

- Repeated increases of > 10 mm Hg for more than 5 minutes following external stimulus
- Baseline intracranial pressure > 10 mm Hg
- Disproportionate increase in intracranial pressure following single environmental stimulus (e.g., nursing maneuver)
- Elevated P_2 intracranial pressure waveform
- Volume-pressure response test variation (volume/pressure ratio 2, pressure/volume index < 10)
- Wide-amplitude intracranial pressure waveform

ETIOLOGICAL OR RELATED FACTORS

- Decreased cerebral perfusion < 50–60 mm Hg
- Sustained increase in intracranial pressure of 10–15 mm Hg
- Systemic hypotension with intracranial hypertension

HIGH-RISK POPULATIONS

- Brain injuries

NOTES

NOTES

NOTES

Sleep-Rest Pattern

Disturbed Sleep Pattern* (Specify Type)

DEFINITION

Time-limited disruption of sleep (natural, periodic suspension of consciousness) time and quality

DEFINING CHARACTERISTICS

Diagnostic Cues

  ♦ Verbal complaints of not feeling well rested

and one or more of the following:

  ♦ Reports interrupted sleep pattern, frequent interruptions during sleep
  ♦ Verbal complaints of difficulty falling asleep (delayed sleep onset)
  ♦ Sleep pattern reversal

Supporting Cues

  ♦ Reports fatigue
  ♦ Reduction in performance (work, school, home)
  ♦ Increasing irritability, restlessness
  ♦ Early awakening
  ♦ Frequent yawning, lethargy
  ♦ Dark circles under eyes
  ♦ Disorientation (progressive)
  ♦ Listlessness
  ♦ Expressionless face
  ♦ Thick speech with mispronunciation and incorrect words
  ♦ Ptosis of eyelids
  ♦ Mild, fleeting nystagmus
  ♦ Slight hand tremor
  ♦ Hallucinations, delirium, paranoia

---

*Diagnosis is very broad. See other diagnoses: Interrupted Sleep Pattern, Sleep-Pattern Reversal, Delayed Sleep Onset, and Sleep Deprivation.

SLEEP-REST PATTERN

ETIOLOGICAL OR RELATED FACTORS

- ◆ Ruminative (over and over) pre-sleep thoughts
- ◆ Physical discomfort (specify)
- ◆ Family stress
- ◆ Environmental or habit changes (social cues)
- ◆ Frequently changing sleep-wake schedule (e.g., shift changes)
- ◆ Daytime boredom, inactivity
- ◆ Fear (specify)
- ◆ Depression
- ◆ Anxiety (personal stress)
- ◆ Pain
- ◆ Perceived vulnerability to harm
- ◆ Nocturia
- ◆ Sustained use of antisleep agents

HIGH-RISK POPULATIONS

- ◆ Around-the-clock therapy (e.g., treatment/medication required during normal sleep time)
- ◆ Nocturnal dyspnea

Sleep Deprivation

DEFINITION
Prolonged periods of time (2 to 3 days or more) without sleep (sustained natural, periodic suspension of relative unconsciousness)

DEFINING CHARACTERISTICS
Diagnostic Cues
+ Verbal report of not feeling well rested
+ Report of less than usual hours of sleep for 2 to 3 days or more (confirmed, if possible)

and one or more of the following:
+ Mood changes
+ Restlessness, irritability, anxiety
+ Fatigue, lethargy, daytime drowsiness
+ Inability to concentrate
+ Inability to concentrate, progressing to deterioration in mental and physical task performance and disorientation
+ Perceptual disorders (e.g., disturbed body sensation, delusions, feeling afloat, hallucinations, acute confusion)
+ Transient paranoia; agitated or combative
+ Mild fleeting nystagmus, hand tremors

ETIOLOGICAL OR RELATED FACTORS
+ Sleep interruptions (specify, e.g., environmental noise)
+ Sustained (unfamiliar or uncomfortable sleep environment)
+ Depression
+ Anxiety; nightmares, sleep terror (children)
+ Fear (specify) or vigilance
+ Pain-management deficit

SLEEP-REST PATTERN

- Drugs (that interfere with sleep)
- Pre-sleep activity or work
- Job stress, frequent shift changes
- Age related sleep stage shifts
- Inadequate daytime activity
- Non-sleep-inducing parenting practices
- Sleep apnea
- Periodic limb movement (e.g., restless leg syndrome, nocturnal myoclonus)
- Sundowners syndrome
- Sleep walking
- Sleep-related painful erections

Delayed Sleep Onset

DEFINITION

Inability to sleep when the expectation is that sleep will occur

DEFINING CHARACTERISTICS

Diagnostic Cues

+ Repeated verbal reports of inability to fall asleep after 30 to 45 minutes of expectation that sleep will occur

Supporting Cues

+ Reports of not feeling well rested
+ Irritability
+ Fatigue
+ Progressing to inability to concentrate, disorientation, and deterioration in mental and physical task performance

ETIOLOGICAL OR RELATED FACTORS

+ Anxiety
+ Fear (specify)
+ Pain-management deficit
+ Drugs
+ Pre-sleep activity or work
+ Job stress
+ Frequent shift changes

Sleep-Pattern Reversal

DEFINITION
Change in sleep-wake cycle from nighttime sleep to predominantly daytime sleep

DEFINING CHARACTERISTICS
Diagnostic Cues
+ Frequent sleep periods and napping during daytime combined with inability to sleep at night
+ Alert during nighttime hours (may engage in activities)

Supporting Cues
+ Mood changes
+ Nocturnal irritability

ETIOLOGICAL OR RELATED FACTORS
+ Low daytime physical activity or exercise level
+ Diversional activity deficit
+ Fear or vigilance

HIGH-RISK POPULATIONS
+ Elderly

Readiness for Enhanced Sleep

DEFINITION

Pattern of natural, periodic, suspension of consciousness that provides adequate rest, sustains a desired lifestyle, and can be strengthened

DEFINING CHARACTERISTICS

- Expresses willingness to enhance sleep
- Amount of sleep and REM sleep is congruent with developmental needs
- Expresses a feeling of being rested after sleep
- Follows sleep routines that promote sleep habits
- Occasional or infrequent use of medications to induce sleep

NOTES

NOTES

Cognitive-Perceptual Pattern

Acute Pain (Specify Location)

DEFINITION

Verbal or coded report of the presence of indicators of severe discomfort (pain) with a duration of less than 6 months (specify type and location (joint pain, low back, cervical, knee pain)

DEFINING CHARACTERISTICS
Diagnostic Cues

   ♦ Report of severe discomfort (pain)
and one or more of the following:
   ♦ Guarding behavior, protecting area
   ♦ Muscle tension increased
   ♦ Facial mask of pain (eyes lack luster, "beaten look," fixed or scattered movement, grimace)
   ♦ Restless, irritable
   ♦ Autonomic responses not seen in chronic, stable pain (diaphoresis, blood pressure, and pulse rate change; pupillary dilation; increased or decreased respiratory rate)
   ♦ Distraction behavior (moaning, crying, pacing, seeking out other people and/or activities, restless)
   ♦ Focus on self
   ♦ Narrowed focus (altered time perception, withdrawal from social contact, impaired thought process)
   ♦ Listless to rigid; antalgic positioning to avoid pain

ETIOLOGICAL OR RELATED FACTORS

   ♦ Knowledge deficit (pain management)

HIGH-RISK POPULATIONS

- ◆ Postsurgical (incisional pain)
- ◆ Arthritis (joint pain)
- ◆ Cardiac (chest pain)
- ◆ Injuring agents (biological, chemical, physical, psychological-stress related)
- ◆ Post-trauma, post-injury

Chronic Pain (Specify Location)

DEFINITION

Severe discomfort (pain) with a duration of more than 6 months (specify type and location (joint pain, low back, cervical, knee pain)

DEFINING CHARACTERISTICS

Diagnostic Cues

- Verbal report or observed evidence of severe discomfort (pain)
- Severe discomfort (pain) experienced for more than 6 months

and one or more of the following:

- Guarded movement
- Altered ability to continue previous activities
- Fear of reinjury
- Facial mask (of pain)
- Physical and social withdrawal
- Anorexia
- Weight changes
- Delayed sleep onset, sleep deprivation

ETIOLOGICAL OR RELATED FACTORS

- Knowledge deficit (chronic pain management)

HIGH-RISK POPULATIONS

- Chronic physical, psychosocial disability (specify; e.g., cancer)

Chronic Pain Self-Management *Deficit*

DEFINITION

Lack of use, or insufficient use, of techniques to reduce pain (e.g., pain medication requests, timing, positioning, distraction)

DEFINING CHARACTERISTICS

Diagnostic Cues

+ Communication (verbal or coded) of pain descriptors
+ Delayed requests for medication, lack of use of positioning, distraction, and other pain-management techniques

and one or more of the following:

+ Guarding behavior, protecting area
+ Self-focusing
+ Narrowed focus of attention (e.g., altered time perception, withdrawal from social contact, impaired thought process)
+ Distraction behavior (moaning, crying, pacing, seeking out other people and/or activities, restless)
+ Facial mask of pain (eyes lack luster, "beaten look," fixed or scattered movement, grimace)
+ Muscle tone listless to rigid

ETIOLOGICAL OR RELATED FACTORS

+ Insufficient knowledge (specify)

HIGH-RISK POPULATIONS

+ Postsurgical (incisional pain; phantom pain)
+ Arthritis (joint pain)
+ Cardiac (chest pain)
+ Injuring agents (biological, chemical, physical, psychological-stress related)
+ Post-trauma

Uncompensated Sensory Loss (Specify Type/Degree)*

DEFINITION

Uncompensated decrease in visual, hearing, touch, smell, or kinesthetic acuity (specify degree of loss)

DEFINING CHARACTERISTICS

Diagnostic Cues

- ◆ Vision—Inability to read newsprint or identify objects and persons
- ◆ Hearing—Inability to identify whispered sounds or normally voiced words
- ◆ Touch—Inability to discriminate various qualities or tactile sensations or absence of tactile perception
- ◆ Smell—Inability to identify odors
- ◆ Kinesthesia—Inability to identify extent, direction, or weight of movement of body or body part

*This condition is frequently a focus for intervention (i.e., an etiological/related factor).

230

Sensory Overload

DEFINITION

Environmental stimuli greater than habitual level of input
and/or monotonous environmental stimuli

DEFINING CHARACTERISTICS

Diagnostic Cues

+ Perceptual distortions of sensory stimuli
+ Amount or complexity of sensory stimuli exceeds the
  usual or desired level, either periodic or continuous
  stimuli
+ Presence of uninterrupted intense and/or unchanging
  stimuli (motor, monitor, light, voices)

Supporting Cues

+ Reduction in reasoning, problem-solving ability,
  and/or work performance
+ Reports sleep disturbances, nightmares
+ Disorientation (periodic or general)
+ Short attention span
+ Restlessness, increased muscle tension
+ Reports fatigue
+ Irritability, anxiety
+ Reports feelings of loss of control

ETIOLOGICAL OR RELATED FACTORS

+ Environmental complexity or monotony

HIGH-RISK POPULATIONS

+ Decreased cognitive capability (head injury)
+ Decreased stress tolerance
+ Intensive care monitoring

Sensory Deprivation

DEFINITION

Reduced environmental and social stimuli relative to habitual (or basic orienting) level

DEFINING CHARACTERISTICS

Diagnostic Cues

- Amount of sensory stimuli less than usual or desired levels (auditory, visual, proprioceptive, reality-orienting, time-orienting input)
- Disorientation or confusion (periodic, general, nocturnal)

and one or more of the following;

- Disorientation
- General, periodic, or nocturnal confusion
- Hallucinations, delirium, paranoia

Supporting Cues

- Apathy
- Anxiety

ETIOLOGICAL OR RELATED FACTORS

- Isolation (restricted environment)
- Therapeutic environmental restriction (specify: isolation, intensive care, bed rest, traction, confining illness, incubator)
- Socially restricted environment (specify: institutionalization, homebound, age debilitation, infant deprivation)
- Uncompensated visual or hearing deficit
- Impaired verbal communication

HIGH-RISK POPULATIONS

- Congenital or acquired sensory loss
- Social isolation
- Therapeutic isolation

Unilateral Neglect*

DEFINITION

Perceptually unaware of and inattentive to one side of the body

DEFINING CHARACTERISTICS

Diagnostic Cues

- Lack of positioning and/or safety precautions in regard to the affected side
- Consistent inattention to stimuli on the affected side:
  - Does not look toward affected side; ignores objects on affected side
  - Leaves food on plate on the affected side

Supporting Cues

- Inadequate self care of affected side

HIGH-RISK POPULATIONS

- Cerebrovascular accident (stroke) or other neurological illness/trauma
- One-sided blindness

*This condition is frequently a focus for intervention (i.e., etiological/related factor).

Knowledge Deficit (Specify Area)*

DEFINITION

Inability to state or explain information or demonstrate a required skill related to disease-management procedures, practices, and/or self care health management (specify area of knowledge deficit, e.g., insulin-dependent diabetic self care, activity prescription, dietary prescription)

DEFINING CHARACTERISTICS
Diagnostic Cues

- Reports inadequate knowledge
- Inadequate recall, understanding, or misinterpretation, misconception of information

and one or more of the following:

- Inadequate performance on a test or demonstration of a skill
- Inaccurate responses to questions
- Unable to follow through after instruction

Supporting Cues

- Requests information
- Does not comply with prescribed health behaviors
- Inappropriate or exaggerated behaviors (e.g., hysterical, hostile, agitated, apathetic)

ETIOLOGICAL OR RELATED FACTORS

- Low readiness for reception of information (anxiety)
- Lack of interest
- Low motivation to learn

Continues

---

*This condition is frequently a focus for intervention (i.e., an etiological/related factor). NANDA International diagnosis is *Deficient Knowledge*.

Knowledge Deficit (Specify Area)—*cont'd*

- Uncompensated memory loss
- Inability to use materials or information resources (e.g., cultural-language differences)
- Unfamiliarity with information resources

HIGH-RISK POPULATIONS

- New treatment regimens
- Complex treatment regimens
- Temporary or permanent cognitive limitations (intellectual)

Readiness for Enhanced Knowledge

DEFINITION

Presence or acquisition of cognitive information related to a specific topic is sufficient for meeting health-related goals and can be strengthened

DEFINING CHARACTERISTICS

- Expresses an interest in learning
- Explains knowledge of the topic
- Behaviors congruent with expressed knowledge
- Describes previous experiences pertaining to the topic

Disturbed Thought Processes*

DEFINITION

Disruption in cognitive operations or activities, relative to chronological age expectation (specify type of alteration; this is a broad taxonomic category)

DEFINING CHARACTERISTICS

Diagnostic Cues

One or more of the following:

- Impaired perception, judgment, decision making
- Impaired attention span; easily distracted
- Impaired ability to grasp ideas (conceptualize) or order ideas (reason and reflection)
- Inappropriate behavior; nonreality-based thinking

Supporting Cues

- Impaired recall ability (see uncompensated memory loss)
- Increased self-concern (egocentricity)
- Hypovigilance or hypervigilance

ETIOLOGICAL OR RELATED FACTORS

- Sensory overload (environmental complexity)
- Delayed developmental progression
- Severe anxiety or depression

HIGH-RISK POPULATIONS

- Dementia; Alzheimer's disease
- Urinary tract infection (older adult)
- Fluid and/or electrolyte imbalance
- Head injury
- Alcohol or drug abuse

*See also Acute/Chronic Confusion, Impaired Environmental Interpretation Syndrome, Uncompensated Memory Loss, Impaired Memory, Risk for Cognitive Impairment.

Attention-Concentration Deficit

DEFINITION

Inability to sustain a focal awareness

DEFINING CHARACTERISTICS

Diagnostic Cues

- Unable to attend to a task for any prolonged period (e.g., more than 5 minutes)
- Easily distracted by any stimulation
- Lack of focus

Supporting Cues

- Inability to block stimuli
- Increased sensitivity to stimuli
- Restlessness
- Confusion
- Agitation, frustration, and/or anger

HIGH-RISK POPULATIONS

- Brain injured
- Alzheimer's disease

Acute Confusion

DEFINITION

Abrupt onset of global, transient changes and disturbances in attention, cognition, psychomotor activity, level of consciousness, and/or sleep-wake cycle

DEFINING CHARACTERISTICS

- Fluctuation in cognition
- Fluctuation in sleep-wake cycle
- Fluctuation in level of consciousness
- Fluctuation in psychomotor activity
- Increased agitation or restlessness
- Misperceptions
- Lack of motivation to initiate and/or follow through with goal-directed or purposeful behavior
- Hallucinations

ETIOLOGICAL OR RELATED FACTORS

- Alcohol abuse
- Drug abuse
- Delirium

HIGH-RISK POPULATIONS

- Dementia
- Over 60 years of age

Chronic Confusion

DEFINITION

Irreversible long-standing and/or progressive deterioration of intellect and personality, characterized by decreased ability to interpret environmental stimuli and decreased capacity for intellectual thought processes, and manifested by disturbances of memory, orientation, and behavior

DEFINING CHARACTERISTICS

- Clinical evidence of organic impairment
- Altered interpretation or response to stimuli
- Progressive or long-standing cognitive impairment
- No change in level of consciousness
- Impaired socialization
- Impaired memory (short term, long term)
- Altered personality

HIGH-RISK POPULATIONS

- Alzheimer's disease
- Korsakoff's psychosis
- Multi-infarct dementia
- Cerebral vascular accident
- Head injury
- Over 60 years of age
- Delirium

Impaired Environmental Interpretation Syndrome

DEFINITION

Consistent lack of orientation to person, place, time, or circumstances over more than 3 to 6 months that necessitates a protective environment

DEFINING CHARACTERISTICS

- Consistent disorientation in known and unknown environments for more than 3 to 6 months
- Chronic confusional states
- Loss of occupational or social functioning from memory decline
- Inability to follow simple directions, instructions
- Inability to reason
- Inability to concentrate
- Slow in responding to questions

ETIOLOGICAL OR RELATED FACTORS

- Depression
- Alcoholism

HIGH-RISK POPULATIONS

- Dementia (Alzheimer's, multi-infarct dementia, Pick's disease, AIDS dementia)
- Parkinson's disease
- Huntington's disease

Uncompensated Memory Loss

DEFINITION

Impaired ability to recall recent events and activities

DEFINING CHARACTERISTICS

Diagnostic Cues

- Frequent episodes of inability to recall recent events, information received, and/or activities, names, places
- Lack of use (or unsuccessful use) of devices or procedures to support memory

Supporting Cues

- Inability to recall previously learned activities, names, places
- Begins an activity and unable to recall intention seconds or minutes later
- Lack of understanding and problem solving based on deficit in short-term recall (minutes, hours)

HIGH-RISK POPULATIONS

- Alzheimer's disease
- Degenerative neurological conditions

Impaired Memory

DEFINITION

Inability to remember or recall bits of information or behavioral skills (impaired memory may be attributed to pathophysiological or situational causes that are either temporary or permanent)

DEFINING CHARACTERISTICS

- Observed or reported experiences of forgetting
- Inability to determine if a behavior was performed
- Inability to learn or retain new skills or information
- Inability to perform a previously learned skill
- Inability to recall factual information
- Inability to recall recent or past events
- Forgetting to perform a behavior at a scheduled time

ETIOLOGICAL OR RELATED FACTORS

- Acute or chronic hypoxia
- Anemia
- Decreased cardiac output
- Fluid and electrolyte imbalance
- Neurological disturbances
- Excessive environmental disturbances

Risk for Cognitive Impairment

DEFINITION

Presence of risk factors for impairment in memory, reasoning ability, judgment, and decision making

RISK FACTORS

- Receiving tranquilizers, sedatives
- Low self-initiative in providing cognitive stimulation
- Borderline neurophysiological pathology
- Confinement to environment low in cognitive stimulation (perceptual, problem solving, decision making)
- Hearing and/or vision deficit combined with decreased stimulation and/or relocation

Decisional Conflict (Specify)

DEFINITION

Uncertainty about course of action to be taken when choice among competing actions involves risk, loss, or challenge to personal life values (specify focus of conflict, e.g., surgery, therapy, abortion, divorce, or other life events)

DEFINING CHARACTERISTICS

Diagnostic Cues

- Delayed decision making and/or vacillation between alternative choices
- Verbalized uncertainty about choices
- Verbalized feeling of distress while attempting a decision
- Physical signs of distress or tension (e.g., increased heart rate, increased muscle tension, or restlessness)

Supporting Cues

- Verbalization of undesired consequences of alternative actions being considered
- Questioning personal values and beliefs while attempting to make a decision
- Self-focusing

ETIOLOGICAL OR RELATED FACTORS

- Perceived threat to value system
- Unclear personal values or beliefs
- Lack of experience or interference with decision making; lack of relevant information; multiple or divergent information sources
- Support system deficit

HIGH-RISK POPULATIONS

- Relocation decisions (e.g., nursing home, moving)
- Terminal illness (treatment preferences)
- Surgical or treatment choices
- Abusive situations

NOTES

NOTES

NOTES

Self-Perception–
Self-Concept Pattern

Fear (Specify Focus)*

DEFINITION

Feeling of dread related to an identifiable source that is perceived as a threat or danger to the self (specify focus; e.g., prognosis, surgical outcome, death, disability)

DEFINING CHARACTERISTICS

Diagnostic Cues

+ Report of feelings of dread, nervousness, or worry/concern about a threatening event, person, or object with expectation of danger to the self
+ Describes (with or without assistance) the focus of perceived threat or danger (potential, actual, or imagined)
+ Narrowing focus of attention progressing to fixed (increased severity)

and one or more of the following:

+ Restlessness; fidgeting
+ Increased questioning or information seeking
+ Increased heart rate, increased respiratory rate
+ Increased muscle tension
+ Increase in quantity or rate of verbalization
+ Vigilance, scanning surroundings
+ Voice tremors, pitch changes
+ Hand tremor
+ Diaphoresis
+ Diminished productivity
+ Irritability

*This condition is frequently a focus for intervention (i.e., etiological/related factor).

SELF-PERCEPTION–SELF-CONCEPT PATTERN

Severe

- ◆ Anguish
- ◆ Uncertainty
- ◆ Distress
- ◆ Sleep disturbance
- ◆ Confusion (elderly)

ETIOLOGICAL OR RELATED FACTORS

- ◆ Knowledge deficit; unfamiliarity with environmental experience(s)
- ◆ Perceived inability to control events (see Powerlessness)
- ◆ Language barrier
- ◆ Sensory impairment (specify)
- ◆ Phobic stimulus

HIGH-RISK POPULATIONS

- ◆ Surgical or diagnostic procedures
- ◆ Surgical outcome
- ◆ First hospitalization
- ◆ Discharge to self care
- ◆ Support system deficit (in stressful situation)

253

Anxiety

DEFINITION

Vague, uneasy feeling of discomfort or dread, the source of which is often nonspecific or unknown to the individual

DEFINING CHARACTERISTICS

Diagnostic Cues

- Reports feeling "anxious," apprehensive, tense, scared, worried, "fearful"
- Reports vague, uneasy feeling of concern about unspecified consequences or changes in life events

and one or more of the following:

- Reports inability to relax, feeling jittery
- Increased muscle tension, foot shuffling, hand or arm movements, trembling, hand tremor, shakiness
- Facial tension
- Lack of concentration
- Insomnia
- Sympathetic response (increased heart rate, respiratory rate, dilated pupils)

Supporting Cues

- Focus on self
- Verbalizes painful and persistent feelings of increased helplessness, inadequacy, regret (see also Ineffective Coping)
- Restlessness, fidgeting, increased perspiration
- Overexcited, rattled, jittery, scared
- Increased wariness, glancing about, poor eye contact, facial tension, voice quivering
- Diminished productivity
- Scanning the environment; vigilance; impaired attention
- Irritability, anguish, distress

SELF-PERCEPTION–SELF-CONCEPT PATTERN

ETIOLOGICAL OR RELATED FACTORS

- Perceived threat to self concept, health status, socioeconomic status, role functioning, interaction patterns, or environment
- Unconscious conflict (essential values or life goals)
- Unmet needs (specify)
- Interpersonal transmission or contagion
- Uncertainty

Mild Anxiety

DEFINITION

Increased level of arousal associated with expectation of a threat (unfocused) to the self or significant relationships

DEFINING CHARACTERISTICS

+ Verbalizes feelings of increased arousal, concern, vigilance
+ Increased questioning
+ Increased awareness
+ Increased attending
+ Mild restlessness
+ Lip chewing, nail biting, foot movements, finger or pencil tapping

ETIOLOGICAL OR RELATED FACTORS

+ Perceived threat to self concept, health status, socioeconomic status, role functioning, interaction patterns, or environment
+ Unconscious conflict (essential values or life goals)
+ Unmet needs (specify)
+ Interpersonal transmission or contagion

Moderate Anxiety

DEFINITION

Increased level of arousal with selective attention and associated with expectation of a threat (unfocused) to the self or significant relationships

DEFINING CHARACTERISTICS

- Expressed feelings of unfocused apprehension, nervousness, or concern
- Verbalizes expectation of danger
- Voice tremors, pitch changes, hand tremor
- Narrowing focus of attention
- Increased rate of verbalization
- Restlessness, pacing, increased muscle tension
- Diaphoresis
- Increased heart and respiratory rate
- Sleep or eating disturbances

ETIOLOGICAL OR RELATED FACTORS

- Separation (use separation anxiety)
- Perceived threat to self concept, health status, socioeconomic status, role functioning, interaction patterns, or environment
- Unconscious conflict (essential values or life goals)
- Unmet needs (specify)
- Interpersonal transmission or contagion

Severe Anxiety (Panic)

DEFINITION

Extreme arousal and scattered focus associated with expectation of a threat to the self or to significant relationships

DEFINING CHARACTERISTCS

- Feelings of unfocused and severe dread, apprehension, nervousness, or concern
- Inappropriate verbalization or absence of verbalization
- Diminished ability to problem solve
- Purposeless activity or immobilization
- Perceptual focus scattered or fixed, or inability to focus on reality
- Increased heart rate
- Hyperventilation
- Diaphoresis
- Increased muscle tension
- Dilated pupils
- Pallor

ETIOLOGICAL OR RELATED FACTORS

- Perceived threat to self concept, health status, socioeconomic status, role functioning, interaction patterns, or environment
- Unconscious conflict (essential values or life goals)
- Unmet needs (specify)
- Interpersonal transmission or contagion

Anticipatory Anxiety (Mild, Moderate, Severe)

DEFINITION

Increased level of arousal associated with a perceived future threat (unfocused) to the self or significant relationships

DEFINING CHARACTERISTICS

Diagnostic Cues

+ Reports feeling anxious, apprehensive, jittery, tense, or fearful
+ Reports vague, uneasy feeling about unspecified future or impending event perceived as a threat to the self or significant relationships (unfocused)

and one or more of the following:

+ Inability to relax
+ Increased muscle tension, restless, foot shuffling, hand or arm movements, trembling
+ Sympathetic response (increased heart rate, respiratory rate, pupils dilated)

ETIOLOGICAL OR RELATED FACTORS

+ Perceived threat to self concept, health status, socioeconomic status, role functioning, interaction patterns, or environment
+ Unconscious conflict (essential values or life goals)
+ Unmet needs (specify)
+ Interpersonal transmission or contagion

Death Anxiety

DEFINITION

Expression of apprehension, worry, or "fear" related to death or dying

DEFINING CHARACTERISTICS

- Expresses deep sadness
- Fear of developing a terminal illness

Concerns: Others

- Worrying about the impact of own death on significant others
- Concerns about overworking the caregiver as terminal illness incapacitates self
- Worrying about being the cause of others' grief and suffering
- Fear of leaving family alone after death

Concerns: Dying Process

- Expresses "fear" of the process of dying
- Powerlessness (issues related to dying)
- Expresses "fear" of loss of physical and/or mental abilities when dying
- Anticipation of pain related to dying
- Expresses concern over total loss of control over any aspect of own death
- Negative death images or unpleasant thoughts about any event related to death and dying
- Fear of delayed demise
- Fear of premature death because it prevents the accomplishment of important life goals

After-Death Concerns

- Concern about meeting one's creator or feeling doubtful about the existence of a god or higher being
- Denial of own mortality or impending death

ETIOLOGICAL OR RELATED FACTORS

To be developed.

Reactive Depression (Specify Focus)

DEFINITION

Acute decrease in self-esteem, worth, or competency linked to a situational threat (specify situational threat; e.g., health outcome, disability, physical deterioration)

DEFINING CHARACTERISTICS

Diagnostic Cues

- Expressions of sadness, despair, or hopelessness about a situation (specify situation)
- Continual questioning of self-worth (self-esteem) or feeling of failure (real or imagined)
- Pessimistic outlook

and one or more of the following to determine severity:

- Withdrawal from others to avoid possible rejection (real or imagined)
- Suspicion or sensitivity to words and actions of others related to general lack of trust of others
- Threats or attempts to commit suicide (refer for immediate evaluation, if observed)
- Extreme dependency on others with related feelings of helplessness and anger
- Misdirected anger (toward self)
- General irritability
- Guilt feelings
- Inability to concentrate on reading, writing, conversation
- Change (usually decrease) in physical activities, eating, sleeping, sexual activity
- Early morning awakening

SELF-PERCEPTION–SELF-CONCEPT PATTERN

ETIOLOGICAL OR RELATED FACTORS

- Perceived powerlessness
- Anxiety

HIGH-RISK POPULATIONS

- Debilitating surgery or trauma, new physical disability
- Significant personal loss

Risk for Loneliness

DEFINITION

Risk for experiencing vague dysphoria

RISK FACTORS

- ◆ Affectional deprivation
- ◆ Physical isolation
- ◆ Cathectic deprivation
- ◆ Social isolation

Hopelessness*

DEFINITION

Perception of limited or no alternatives or personal choices available and unable to mobilize energy on own behalf

DEFINING CHARACTERISTICS

Diagnostic Cues

- Verbalization of despondent or hopeless content (e.g., "I can't," sighing; feel empty, drained; "end of my rope," feeling of deprivation, impossibility)
- Lack of initiative or ambition (e.g., lack of involvement in care; passively allowing care)
- Decreased affect

and one or more of the following:

- General passivity; decreased verbalization
- Decreased appetite
- Increased sleep time
- Shrugging in response to speaker
- Closing eyes
- Turning away from speaker
- Decreased response to stimuli
- Expresses the perception of no alternatives (severe)

ETIOLOGICAL OR RELATED FACTORS

- Prolonged activity restriction (creating isolation)
- Abandonment
- Loss of belief (transcendent values or god)

Continues

---

*See also Powerlessness, Situational Depression.

Hopelessness—*cont'd*

HIGH-RISK POPULATIONS

- Impaired adjustment to chronic or terminal illness (self or significant other)
- Chronic pain
- Self care or mobility deficits
- Activity intolerance
- History of long-term stress
- Failing or deteriorating physiological condition
- Long-term stress

Powerlessness (Severe, Moderate, Low)*

DEFINITION

Perceived lack of control over a situation and perception that own actions will not significantly affect an outcome

DEFINING CHARACTERISTICS

Diagnostic Cues

Severe

- ♦ Verbalization of having no control or influence over a situation, an outcome(s), or self care
- ♦ Does not participate in health care decisions
- ♦ Apathy

Supporting Cues

Severe

- ♦ Depressed over physical deterioration despite compliance with regimens

Moderate

- ♦ Passivity

and one or more of the following:

- ♦ Expressed doubt regarding role performance
- ♦ Expressed dissatisfaction or frustration over inability to perform previous roles, tasks, activities
- ♦ Dependence on others that may result in irritability, resentment, anger, guilt
- ♦ Nonparticipation in care or decision making when opportunities provided

Continues

*See also Reactive Depression, Hopelessness.

Powerlessness (Severe, Moderate, Low)—*cont'd*

- Reluctance to express true feelings fearing alienation from caregivers
- Does not monitor progress, seek information regarding care, or defend self care practices when challenged

Low

- Expressed uncertainty about fluctuating energy levels

ETIOLOGICAL OR RELATED FACTORS

- Health care environment (specify aspect)
- Perceived interpersonal control by others
- Lifestyle of helplessness
- Impaired verbal communication

HIGH-RISK POPULATIONS

- Degenerative disease
- Forced relocation
- Institutional residency

Risk for Powerlessness

DEFINITION

At risk for perceived lack of control over a situation and/or ability to significantly affect an outcome

RISK FACTORS

Physiological

- ◆ Chronic or acute illness (hospitalization, intubation, ventilator, suctioning)
- ◆ Acute injury or progressive debilitating disease process (e.g., spinal cord injury, multiple sclerosis)
- ◆ Aging (e.g., decreased physical strength, decreased mobility)
- ◆ Dying

Psychosocial

- ◆ Lack of knowledge of illness or health care system
- ◆ Lifestyle of dependency with inadequate coping patterns
- ◆ Describes feeling of inability to influence events
- ◆ Decreased self-esteem
- ◆ Low or unstable body image

Chronic Low Self-Esteem*

DEFINITION

Long-standing negative self-evaluation or feelings about self or self-capabilities, which may be directly or indirectly expressed

DEFINING CHARACTERISTICS

Diagnostic Cues

- ♦ All behaviors below are long-standing or chronic:
    - ♦ Repeated self-negating verbalizations
    - ♦ Lack of eye contact, head flexion, and/or shoulder flexion

Supporting Cues

- ♦ Evaluations of self as unable to deal with events
- ♦ Hesitation to try new things or situations
- ♦ Exaggerations of negative feedback about self
- ♦ Rationalizations or rejections of positive feedback
- ♦ Frequent lack of success in work or other life events
- ♦ Overly conforming, dependent on others' opinions
- ♦ Nonassertive or passive
- ♦ Indecisive
- ♦ Excessively seeking reassurance
- ♦ Expressions of shame or guilt
- ♦ High level of negative criticism from significant other

*This condition is frequently a focus for intervention (e.g., etiological/related factors).

SELF-PERCEPTION–SELF-CONCEPT PATTERN

Situational Low Self-Esteem*

DEFINITION

Development of a negative perception of self-worth in response to a current situation

DEFINING CHARACTERISTICS

Diagnostic Cues

- ◆ Repeated self-negating verbalizations (negative feelings about self)
- ◆ Evaluation of self as unable to deal with situations or events

and one or more of the following:

- ◆ Lack of eye contact
- ◆ Head flexion
- ◆ Shoulder flexion

Supporting Cues

- ◆ Indecisive; nonassertive
- ◆ Hesitation to try new things or situations
- ◆ Rationalizations or rejections of positive feedback
- ◆ Exaggerations of negative feedback about self
- ◆ Hypersensitivity to a slight or a criticism
- ◆ Expressions of shame or guilt
- ◆ Expressions of helplessness and uselessness
- ◆ Compensations:
  - ◆ Grandiosity (see also Defensive Coping)
  - ◆ Denial of problems obvious to others (see also Defensive Coping)
  - ◆ Projection of blame or responsibility for problems (see also Defensive Coping)
  - ◆ Rationalization of personal failures (see also Defensive Coping) *Continues*

*This condition is frequently a focus for intervention (i.e., etiological/related factor).

Situational Low Self-Esteem—*cont'd*

RELATED FACTORS

- ♦ Developmental changes (specify)
- ♦ Disturbed body image
- ♦ Functional impairment (specify)
- ♦ Loss (specify)
- ♦ Social role changes (specify)
- ♦ Lack of recognition/rewards
- ♦ Behavior inconsistent with values
- ♦ Failures/rejections

Risk for Situational Low Self-Esteem

DEFINITION

Presence of risk factors for developing negative perception of self-worth in response to a current situation (specify)

RISK FACTORS

- Developmental changes (specify)
- Disturbed body image
- Functional impairment (specify)
- Loss (specify)
- Social role changes (specify)
- Lack of recognition/rewards
- Behavior inconsistent with values
- Failures/rejections
- Unrealistic self-expectations
- History of abuse, neglect, abandonment

Disturbed Body Image*

DEFINITION

Negative feelings or perceptions about characteristics, functions, or limits of body or body part

DEFINING CHARACTERISTICS

Diagnostic Cues

- ◆ Verbalized actual or perceived change in structure and/or function of body or body part
- ◆ Verbalized feelings of helplessness, hopelessness, and/or powerlessness in relation to body and fear of rejection or reaction of others

and one or more of the following:

- ◆ Verbalized negative feelings about body (e.g., dirty, big, small, unsightly)
- ◆ Repeated expressions of negative feeling about loss of body fluids, addition of body fluids, or machines
- ◆ Repeated verbalizations focusing on past strength, function, or appearance

Supporting Cues

- ◆ Verbalized change in lifestyle because of negative feelings or perceptions of body
- ◆ Preoccupation with change in body or loss of part
- ◆ Refusal to verify actual change in body or body part
- ◆ Change in ability to estimate spatial relationship of body to environment
- ◆ Personalization of part, or loss, by name
- ◆ Depersonalization of part or loss by impersonal pronoun

---

*This condition is frequently a focus for intervention (e.g., etiological/related factors).

- Extension of body boundary to incorporate environmental objects (e.g., machines, oxygen, respirator)
- Emphasis on remaining strengths or heightened achievement
- Trauma to nonfunctioning part (intentional or nonintentional)
- Change in social involvement or social relationships
- Hiding or overexposing body part
- Not touching body part
- Not looking at body part
- Missing body part
- Actual change in structure and/or function of body or body part

ETIOLOGICAL OR RELATED FACTORS

- Nonintegration of change (in body characteristics, function, or limits)
- Perceived developmental imperfections
- Obesity

HIGH-RISK POPULATIONS

- Hemiplegia
- Loss of a body part (e.g., leg amputation, breast removal)
- Loss or change in body function (e.g., reproductive, elimination)
- Facial trauma
- Pacemaker implant
- Congenital anomalies (observable)

Disturbed Personal Identity

DEFINITION

Inability to distinguish between self and nonself

DEFINING CHARACTERISTICS

- Inability to distinguish self from others or objects
- Verbalizations of "not knowing who I am"

Readiness for Enhanced Self Concept

DEFINITION

Pattern of perception or ideas about the self that is sufficient for well-being and can be strengthened

DEFINING CHARACTERISTICS

- Expresses willingness to enhance self concept
- Expresses satisfaction with thoughts about self, sense of worthiness, role performance, body image, and personal identity
- Actions are congruent with expressed feelings and thoughts
- Expresses confidence in abilities
- Accepts strengths and limitations

Risk for Self-Directed Violence

DEFINITION

Presence of risk factors for behavior that can be physically, emotionally, and/or sexually harmful to the self

RISK FACTORS

- Suicidal ideation (frequent, intense, prolonged)
- Suicidal plan (clear and specific lethality; method and availability of destructive means)
- History of multiple suicide attempts; family history of suicide
- Behavioral clues (e.g., writing forlorn love notes, directing angry messages at a significant other who has rejected the person, giving away personal items, taking out a large insurance policy)
- Verbal clues (e.g., talking about death, "better off without me," asking questions about lethal dosages of drugs)
- Emotional status (hopelessness, despair, increased anxiety, panic, anger, hostility)
- Mental health (severe depression, psychosis, severe personality disorder, alcoholism or drug abuse)
- Conflict in interpersonal relationships
- Marital status (single, widowed, divorced)
- Occupation (executive, administrator, owner of business, professional, or semiskilled worker)
- Employment (unemployed, recent job loss/failure)
- Personal resources (poor achievement, poor insight)
- Social resources (poor rapport, socially isolated, unresponsive family)
- Family background (chaotic or conflictual)

SELF-PERCEPTION–SELF-CONCEPT PATTERN

- Engagement in autoerotic sexual acts
- Age 15–19 and over 45
- Sexual orientation (active bisexual, inactive homosexual)

NOTES

NOTES

NOTES

Role-Relationship
Pattern

Anticipatory Grieving*

DEFINITION

Expectation of disruption in a familiar pattern or significant relationships (includes people, possessions, job, status, home, ideals, and parts and processes of the body)

DEFINING CHARACTERISTICS

Diagnostic Cues

+ Potential for loss of significant people, possessions, job, status, home, ideals, and parts and processes of the body
+ Verbal expression of distress at potential (anticipated) loss

and one or more of the following:

+ Anger
+ Sadness, sorrow, crying
+ Crying at frequent intervals, choked feeling
+ Change in eating habits
+ Alteration in sleep or dream patterns
+ Alteration in activity level
+ Altered libido
+ Idealization of anticipated loss
+ Developmental regression
+ Alterations in concentration or pursuit of tasks

*This condition is frequently a focus for intervention (e.g., etiological/related factors).

Dysfunctional Grieving

DEFINITION

Extended length or severity of grieving process (unresolved grieving) following an actual or perceived loss or change in pattern of relationships (includes people, possessions, job, status, home, ideals, and parts and processes of the body)

DEFINING CHARACTERISTICS

Diagnostic Cues

* Verbal expression of distress/despair at a loss or denial of loss

and one of the following:

* Arrested grieving process before resolution
* Prolonged grieving beyond expected time for cultural group
* Emotional response more exaggerated than expected for cultural group (severity of reaction)

Supporting Cues

* Alterations in concentration and/or pursuits of tasks
* Expression of guilt, self-criticism
* Expression of unresolved issues
* Sadness, anger, crying, labile affect
* Difficulty in expressing meaning of loss
* Alterations in activities of daily living: work, socialization, altered libido, change in eating habits, sleep-dream pattern
* Idealization of lost object
* Reliving past experiences, developmental regression
* Death anxiety

Continues

Dysfunctional Grieving—*cont'd*

ETIOLOGICAL OR RELATED FACTORS

- Loss or perceived loss or change (specify)
- Unavailable support systems

HIGH-RISK POPULATIONS

- Preloss neuroticism
- Frequent major life events, changes
- History of psychiatric or mental health disorder
- Congenital anomaly
- Perinatal loss (later gestational age, length of life of infant, marital adjustment problems, past perinatal losses, absence of other living children)

Risk for Dysfunctional Grieving

DEFINITION

Presence of risk factors for an extended length or severity of grieving process following actual or perceived loss

RISK FACTORS

- Preloss neuroticism
- Frequent major life events, changes
- Past psychological or psychiatric problems
- Predisposition for anxiety and feelings of inadequacy
- Congenital anomaly
- Perinatal loss (later gestational age, length of life of infant, marital adjustment problems, past perinatal losses, absence of other living children)

Chronic Sorrow

DEFINITION

Cyclical, recurring, and potentially progressive pattern of pervasive sadness, experienced in response to continual loss, throughout the trajectory of a chronic illness or disability

DEFINING CHARACTERISTICS

- ◆ Describes differences or gap between current and former or desired situation
- ◆ Expresses one or more of the following feelings that vary in intensity, are periodic, may progress and intensify over time, and may interfere with the client's ability to reach highest level of personal and social well-being:
  - ◆ Periodic, recurrent feelings of sadness
  - ◆ Anger
  - ◆ Being misunderstood
  - ◆ Confusion
  - ◆ Depression, loneliness, emptiness
  - ◆ Disappointment, frustration
  - ◆ Fear
  - ◆ Guilt or self-blame
  - ◆ Helplessness, hopelessness, overwhelmed
  - ◆ Low self-esteem
  - ◆ Loss (recurring)

ETIOLOGICAL OR RELATED FACTORS

- ◆ Chronic or life-threatening illness or disability (specify mental retardation, multiple sclerosis, infertility, cancer, Parkinson's disease, prematurity, spina bifida or other birth defects, chronic mental illness [e.g., schizophrenia, bipolar disorder, autism, dementia])

ROLE-RELATIONSHIP PATTERN

- Death of a loved one
- One or more trigger events (those circumstances, situations, and conditions that bring the disparity resulting from the loss experience clearly into focus or that exacerbate the experience of disparity):
  - Crises in management of the illness
  - Crises related to developmental stages and missed opportunities or milestones (that bring comparisons with developmental, social, or personal norms)
  - Unending caregiving or other role changes that serve as a constant reminder of disparity between self and others

HIGH-RISK POPULATIONS

- Individual or family caregiver experiencing continual loss throughout the trajectory of a chronic or life-threatening illness
- Bereaved individual in response to loss of a loved one
- Anatomical defect (e.g., cleft palate, altered neuromuscular visual system, auditory system, phonatory apparatus)

Ineffective Role Performance (Specify)

DEFINITION

Change, conflict, denial of role responsibilities or inability to perform role responsibilities (specify type; this is a broad taxonomic category)

DEFINING CHARACTERISTICS

- ◆ Denial of role
- ◆ Conflict in roles
- ◆ Change in self-perception of role
- ◆ Change in others' perception of role
- ◆ Change in physical capacity to resume role
- ◆ Lack of knowledge of role
- ◆ Change in usual patterns of responsibilities:
  - ◆ Role overload
  - ◆ Role dissatisfaction
  - ◆ Role confusion
  - ◆ Role strain
  - ◆ Role ambivalence

Unresolved Independence-Dependence Conflict

DEFINITION

Need and desire to be dependent (or independent) with a therapeutic, maturational, or social expectation to be independent (or dependent)

DEFINING CHARACTERISTICS

Diagnostic Cues

+ Repeated verbal expressions of desire for independence (in situations that require some dependence: therapeutic, maturational, social)

or

+ Repeated verbal expressions of desire for dependence (in situations that require independence; therapeutic, maturational, social)

and one or more of the following:

+ Expression of anger
+ Anxiety

HIGH-RISK POPULATIONS

+ Spinal cord injury
+ Adolescents
+ Bed rest confinement
+ Degenerative chronic disease
+ Physical activity restrictions

Social Isolation or *Social Rejection**

DEFINITION

Condition of aloneness experienced by the individual and perceived as imposed by others and as a negative or threatening state

DEFINING CHARACTERISTICS

Diagnostic Cues

One or more of the following:

- Expresses feelings of aloneness imposed by others, feelings of rejection, feelings of difference from others
- Shows behavior unaccepted by dominant cultural group
- Expresses values acceptable to subculture but unacceptable to dominant cultural group
- Observed or expressed interests or activities inappropriate or not acceptable for the developmental age or stage

Supporting Cues

- Preoccupation with own thoughts, repetitive meaningless actions
- Perceived inability to meet expectations of others or insecurity in public
- Seeks to be alone or to exist in a subculture
- Perceived inadequacy of significant purpose in life or absence of purpose in life
- Sad, dull affect
- Uncommunicative, withdrawn, no eye contact
- Projects hostility in voice, behavior

---

*NANDA International uses the term *social isolation* for this condition.

ROLE-RELATIONSHIP PATTERN

ETIOLOGICAL OR RELATED FACTORS

- Alteration in physical appearance or mental status
- Developmental delay (social skills)
- Immature interests
- Unacceptable social behavior or values
- Altered state of wellness
- Inability to engage in satisfying personal relationships

HIGH-RISK POPULATIONS

- Mental disorders
- Observable disabilities, stigmata
- Retardation

Social Isolation

DEFINITION

Feelings of aloneness attributed to interpersonal interaction below level desired or required for personal integrity

DEFINING CHARACTERISTICS

Diagnostic Cues

◆ Verbalization of isolation from others

and one or more of the following:

- ◆ Lack of contact with, or absence of, significant others
- ◆ Absent or limited contact with community
- ◆ Low contact with peers

Supporting Cues

- ◆ Apathy
- ◆ Seclusion

ETIOLOGICAL OR RELATED FACTORS

- ◆ Impaired mobility
- ◆ Therapeutic isolation
- ◆ Sociocultural dissonance
- ◆ Insufficient community resources
- ◆ Body image disturbance
- ◆ Fear (environmental hazards, violence)

HIGH-RISK POPULATIONS

- ◆ Frail elderly
- ◆ Therapeutic isolation
- ◆ Disfigurement

Impaired Social Interaction

DEFINITION

Insufficient or excessive quantity or ineffective quality of social exchange

DEFINING CHARACTERISTICS

Diagnostic Cues

- Verbalized or observed discomfort in social situations (e.g., inability to receive or communicate a satisfying sense of belonging, caring, interest, or shared history)
- Observed use of unsuccessful social interaction behaviors

Supporting Cues

- Dysfunctional interaction with peers, family, others
- Family report of change of style or patterns of interaction

ETIOLOGICAL OR RELATED FACTORS

- Knowledge or skill deficit (ways to enhance mutuality)
- Communication barriers
- Self concept disturbance
- Absence of available significant others or peers (support system deficit)
- Limited physical mobility
- Therapeutic isolation
- Sociocultural dissonance
- Environmental barriers
- Altered thought processes
- Sensory deficit (vision, hearing)

Developmental Delay: Social Skills (Specify)

DEFINITION

Demonstrates deviations from age-group norms in acquisition of social skills

DEFINING CHARACTERISTICS

Diagnostic Cues

- Delay or difficulty in acquisition of social interaction skills typical of age-group or developmental level
- Dysfunctional interactions

ETIOLOGICAL OR RELATED FACTORS

- Environmental, stimulation, modeling deficiencies
- Inconsistent responsiveness
- Multiple caretakers, inadequate caretaking
- Separation (from significant others)
- Physical disability effects
- Indifference
- Self-esteem disturbance
- Social isolation

Relocation Stress Syndrome*

DEFINITION

Physiological and psychosocial disturbances resulting from transfer from one environment to another

DEFINING CHARACTERISTICS

Diagnostic Cues

- Change in environment or location
- Anxiety, apprehension, verbalization of being concerned or upset about transfer
- Reactive depression, sad affect and/or increased confusion (elderly population)
- Expressions of loneliness
- Feeling of powerlessness or anger regarding move
- Sleep pattern disturbance and/or change in eating habits, gastrointestinal disturbances

Supporting Cues

- Moderate to high degree of environment change
- Unfavorable comparison of posttransfer with pretransfer staff
- Little or no preparation for impending move
- History of previous transfers (same or different type)
- Losses involved with decision to move
- Concurrent, recent, past losses
- Dependency
- Insecurity, lack of trust
- Support system deficit
- Restlessness, vigilance, or withdrawal

Continues

---

*Generally, the probable cause (related or etiological factors) of a syndrome is contained in the name (e.g., relocation).

Relocation Stress Syndrome—*cont'd*

- Weight change
- Impaired or decreased health status (psychosocial/physical)

HIGH-RISK POPULATIONS

- Lack of predeparture counseling/support
- Language barrier
- Isolation from family/friends
- Unstable health status

Risk for Relocation Stress Syndrome

DEFINITION

Risk for physiological and psychosocial disturbances resulting from transfer from one environment to another

RISK FACTORS

- Moderate to high degree of environmental change (e.g., physical, ethnic, cultural)
- Temporary or permanent move
- Voluntary or involuntary move
- Lack of adequate support system/group
- Moderate mental competence (e.g., alert enough to experience changes)
- Unpredictability of experiences
- Decreased psychosocial or physical health status
- Lack of predeparture counseling
- Passive coping
- Past or current losses

Interrupted Family Processes (Specify)

DEFINITION

Inability of family system (household members) to meet needs of members, carry out family functions, or maintain communications for mutual growth and maturation

DEFINING CHARACTERISTICS

- ♦ Inability of family members to relate to each other for mutual growth and maturation
- ♦ Failure to send and receive clear messages
- ♦ Poorly communicated family rules, rituals, symbols; unexamined myths
- ♦ Unhealthy family decision-making processes
- ♦ Inability of family members to express and accept wide range of feelings
- ♦ Inability to accept and receive help
- ♦ Does not demonstrate respect for individuality and autonomy of members
- ♦ Rigidity in functions and roles
- ♦ Fails to accomplish current (or past) family developmental tasks
- ♦ Inappropriate (nonproductive) boundary maintenance
- ♦ Inability to adapt to change
- ♦ Inability to deal with traumatic or crisis experience constructively
- ♦ Parents do not demonstrate respect for each other's views on child-rearing practices
- ♦ Inappropriate (nonproductive) level and direction of energy
- ♦ Inability to meet needs of members (physical, security, emotional, spiritual)
- ♦ Family uninvolved in community activities

ROLE-RELATIONSHIP PATTERN

ETIOLOGICAL OR RELATED FACTORS

- Situational crisis or transition (e.g., alcoholism of a member)
- Developmental crisis or transition

Dysfunctional Family Processes: Alcoholism

DEFINITION

Psychosocial, spiritual, and physiological functions of family unit are chronically disorganized, leading to conflict, denial of problems, resistance to change, ineffective problem solving, and a series of self-perpetuating crises

DEFINING CHARACTERISTICS

Diagnostic Cues

Roles and Relationships

- Deterioration in family relationships, disturbed family dynamics
- Ineffective spouse communication or marital problems
- Altered role function or disruption of family roles
- Inconsistent parenting or low perception of parental support
- Family denial
- Intimacy dysfunction, difficulty with intimate relationships
- Chronic family problems
- Closed communication systems

Behaviors

- Inappropriate expression of anger
- Loss of control of drinking
- Impaired communication
- Ineffective problem-solving skills
- Rationalization or denial of problems
- Enabling to maintain drinking
- Inability to meet emotional needs of family members
- Manipulation
- Dependency

- Criticizing
- Alcohol abuse
- Broken promises
- Refusal to get help or inability to accept and receive help appropriately
- Blaming
- Inadequate understanding or knowledge of alcoholism

Feelings

- Decreased self-esteem, worthlessness, insecurity
- Anger or suppressed rage
- Frustration, powerlessness, hopelessness
- Anxiety, tension, distress
- Repressed emotions
- Responsibility for alcoholic's behavior
- Lingering resentment, hurt, shame, embarrassment
- Unhappiness, emotional isolation, loneliness, rejection
- Guilt
- Vulnerability
- Mistrust

Supporting Cues

Roles and Relationships

- Triangulating family relationships
- Reduced ability of family members to relate to each other for mutual growth and maturation
- Lack of skills necessary for relationships
- Lack of cohesiveness, disrupted family rituals
- Family unable to meet security needs of its members, pattern of rejection
- Family does not demonstrate respect for individuality and autonomy of its members
- Economic problems, neglected obligations

Continues

Dysfunctional Family Processes: Alcoholism—*cont'd*

Behaviors

- Inability to meet spiritual needs of its members
- Inability to express or accept wide range of feelings
- Orientation toward tension relief rather than achievement of goals
- Family special occasions are alcohol centered
- Escalating conflict
- Lying
- Contradictory, paradoxical communication
- Lack of dealing with conflict
- Harsh self-judgment
- Isolation
- Substance abuse other than alcohol or nicotine addiction
- Difficulty having fun
- Self-blaming
- Unresolved grief
- Controlling communication or power struggles
- Inability to adapt to change
- Immaturity
- Stress-related physical illnesses
- Inability to deal with traumatic experiences constructively
- Seeking approval and affirmation
- Lack of reliability
- Disturbances in academic performance in children
- Disturbances in concentration
- Chaos
- Failure to accomplish current or past developmental tasks and difficulty with life cycle transitions
- Verbal abuse of spouse or parent
- Agitation
- Diminished physical contact

Feelings

- Being different from other people
- Depression
- Hostility
- Emotional control by others
- Confusion, lack of identity
- Dissatisfaction, moodiness
- Loss, abandonment
- Misunderstood
- Confused love and pity
- Failure, being unloved

ETIOLOGICAL OR RELATED FACTORS

- Abuse of alcohol, resistance to treatment
- Family history of alcoholism
- Inadequate coping skills
- Genetic predisposition, addictive personality
- Lack of problem-solving skills

Readiness for Enhanced Family Processes

DEFINITION

Pattern of family functioning that is sufficient to support the well-being of family members and can be strengthened

DEFINING CHARACTERISTICS

- Expresses desire to enhance family dynamics
- Family functioning meets physical, social, and psychological needs of family members
- Activities support the safety and growth of family members
- Communication is adequate
- Relationships are generally positive; interdependent with community; family tasks are accomplished
- Family roles are flexible and appropriate for developmental stages
- Respect for family members is evident
- Family adapts to change
- Boundaries of family members are maintained
- Energy level of family supports activities of daily living
- Family resilience is evident
- Balance exists between autonomy and cohesiveness

Impaired Parenting (Specify Impairment)

DEFINITION

Inability of the primary caretaker to create an environment that promotes the optimal growth and development of the child (adjustment to parenting, in general, is a normal maturation process following the birth of a child)

DEFINING CHARACTERISTICS

Parental

- ♦ Insecure attachment or lack of attachment to infant
- ♦ Maternal-child or parent-child interaction deficit
- ♦ Inability to recognize and act on infant cues
- ♦ Inconsistent or inappropriate caretaking skills:
  - ♦ Inconsistent behavior management
  - ♦ Inconsistent care
  - ♦ Inappropriate child care arrangements
  - ♦ Inflexibility to meet needs of child, situation
  - ♦ Inadequate child health maintenance
- ♦ Inappropriate visual, tactile, auditory stimulation:
  - ♦ Negative statements about child
  - ♦ Rejection of or hostility toward child
  - ♦ Highly punitive
  - ♦ Little cuddling
  - ♦ Abandonment
  - ♦ Child abuse
  - ♦ Child neglect
  - ♦ Preference for physical punishment
- ♦ Unrealistic expectations of child, self, partner
- ♦ Unsafe home environment
- ♦ Statements of inability to meet child's needs
- ♦ Verbalization that cannot control child
- ♦ Verbalizations of role inadequacy, frustration

Continues

Impaired Parenting (Specify Impairment)—cont'd

Infant or Child

- Failure to thrive
- Lack of attachment (e.g., lack of separation anxiety)
- Poor cognitive development, poor academic performance
- Poor social competence
- Behavioral disorders, frequent illnesses, accidents
- Evidence of abuse
- Runaway

ETIOLOGICAL OR RELATED FACTORS

Physical Factors

- Sleep deprivation or disruption
- Infant or child handicapping condition or developmental delay

Social Factors

- Not gender desired
- Parent-infant or parent-child prolonged separation
- Attention deficit–hyperactivity disorder
- Lack of fit between temperament of child and parental expectations
- Father of child not involved
- Marital conflict, declining satisfaction
- Lack of family cohesiveness
- Financial difficulties, poverty
- Unemployment or job problems
- Lack of resources or lack of access to resources (e.g., transportation)
- Legal difficulties
- Lack of or poor parental role model
- Poor home environment

- Relocations
- Change in family unit
- Lack of value of parenthood
- Social isolation, social support network deficit
- Stress
- Role strain or overload
- Maladaptive coping strategies
- Poor problem-solving skills or communication skills
- Low self-esteem
- Inability to put child's needs before own

Knowledge Factors

- Knowledge deficit (child development)
- Knowledge (parenting skills)
- Knowledge deficit (child health maintenance)
- Lack of cognitive readiness for parenthood
- Low cognitive functioning
- Poor communication skills

HIGH-RISK POPULATIONS

- Disability
- Single parents
- Low socioeconomic class
- Low educational level or attainment
- History of being abused
- History of being abusive
- History of substance abuse, dependencies, mental illness
- Unplanned or unwanted pregnancy
- Premature birth; difficult labor and delivery
- Young age, especially adolescent
- High number of closely spaced pregnancies
- Lack of or late prenatal care
- Multiple births
- Parent-infant separation at birth

Risk for Impaired Parenting (Specify)

DEFINITION

Risk for inability of primary caretaker to create, maintain, or regain an environment that promotes the optimal growth and development of the child (adjustment to parenting, in general, is a normal maturation process following the birth of a child)

RISK FACTORS

Social Factors

+ Single parent
+ Father of child not involved
+ Lack of family cohesiveness
+ Poverty
+ Financial difficulties
+ Unemployment or job problems
+ Low socioeconomic class
+ Lack of resources and/or access to resources (e.g., transportation)
+ History of being abused
+ History of being abusive
+ Legal difficulties
+ Lack of or poor parental role model
+ Poor home environment
+ Relocation
+ Change in family unit
+ Lack of value of parenthood
+ Social isolation, social support network deficit
+ Role strain or overload
+ Maladaptive coping strategies or stress
+ Poor problem-solving or communication skills
+ Low self-esteem

- Inability to put child's needs before own
- Unplanned or unwanted pregnancy
- Inadequate child care arrangements

Knowledge Factors

- Unrealistic expectations of child
- Knowledge deficit (child development)
- Knowledge deficit (parenting skills)
- Knowledge deficit (child health maintenance)
- Lack of cognitive readiness for parenthood
- Low educational level or attainment, low cognitive functioning
- Inability to recognize and act on infant cues
- Preference for physical punishment

Physical Factors

- Lack of or late prenatal care
- Young age, especially adolescent
- High number of closely spaced children
- Multiple birth
- Difficult labor and/or delivery
- Physical illness, disability
- Sleep deprivation or disruption

Psychological Factors

- Marital conflict, declining satisfaction
- Separation from infant or child
- History of substance abuse or dependence
- History of mental illness
- Depression

Infant/Child Factors

- Separation from parent at birth
- Prolonged separation from parent

Continues

Risk for Impaired Parenting (Specify)—*cont'd*

- ◆ Premature birth
- ◆ Infant or child illness
- ◆ Handicapping condition or developmental delay
- ◆ Difficult temperament
- ◆ Lack of goodness of fit (temperament) with parental expectations
- ◆ Attention deficit–hyperactivity disorder
- ◆ Unplanned or unwanted child or not the gender desired
- ◆ Multiple birth
- ◆ Altered perceptual abilities

Parental Role Conflict

DEFINITION

Role confusion and conflict experienced by parent(s) in response to crisis

DEFINING CHARACTERISTICS

Diagnostic Cues

One or more of the following:

- Expresses concerns or feelings of inadequacy to provide for child's physical and emotional needs during hospitalization or in the home; is reluctant to participate in usual caretaking activities, even with encouragement and support
- Expresses concerns about changes in parental role, family functioning, family communication, family health
- Demonstrates disruption in caretaking routines
- Expresses concern about perceived loss of control over decisions relating to child
- Verbalizes or demonstrates feelings of guilt, anger, fear, anxiety, and/or frustrations about effect of a child's illness on family process (see Altered Family Process)

ETIOLOGICAL OR RELATED FACTORS

- Parent-child separation (because of chronic illness)
- Intimidation with invasive or restrictive modalities (e.g., isolation, intubation, specialized care centers, policies)
- Establishing home care of a child with special needs (e.g., apnea monitoring, postural drainage, hyperalimentation)
- Change in marital status
- Interruptions in family life caused by home care regimen (treatments, caregivers, lack of respite)

Weak Parent-Infant Attachment

DEFINITION

Pattern of unreciprocal bonding relationship between parent and infant or primary caretaker and infant

DEFINING CHARACTERISTICS

Diagnostic Cues

Infant

- Infant does not respond to attempts to soothe or satisfy
- Inability of infant to give care-eliciting and/or behavioral cues
- Irritable infant or low responsiveness to parent

Parent-Infant

- Low reciprocal interaction pattern (e.g., minimal smiling, babbling response to touching, kissing)
- Absent or minimal eye contact

Parent

- Infrequent visitation of hospitalized infant (e.g., less than twice a week)
- Minimal smiling, close contact, enfolding, talking to baby
- Minimal touching, stroking, patting, rocking, holding, kissing of infant except when necessary to feed or change diapers
- Inappropriate or lack of parental response to infant cues (e.g., does not attempt comforting responses to crying or continues unsuccessful methods)
- Does not assume "en-face" position, eye-to-eye contact

ROLE-RELATIONSHIP PATTERN

Prenatal

+ Negative or ambivalent feelings regarding pregnancy continuing into third trimester

Supporting Cues

+ Few positive comments about infant, expressions of disappointment
+ Bottle propped or tense posture during breastfeeding
+ Prenatal history of ambivalence, negative or ambivalent feelings regarding pregnancy continuing into third trimester
+ High-risk adolescent parent, physically or mentally ill parent
+ Parental resentment of infant following maternal death or severe illness

ETIOLOGICAL OR RELATED FACTORS

+ Parental anxiety
+ Fear (specify)
+ Parent-infant separation
+ Perceived low parenting competency (infant care)
+ Low (infant) social responsiveness
+ Support system deficit
+ Family stress

Risk for Impaired Parent-Infant/Child Attachment

DEFINITION

Disruption of the interactive process between parent or significant other and infant that fosters the development of a protective and nurturing reciprocal relationship

RISK FACTORS

- Inability of parents to meet personal needs
- Anxiety associated with the parent role
- Substance abuse
- Premature infant
- Ill infant or child who is unable to effectively initiate parental contact because of altered behavioral organization
- Parent-infant separation
- Physical barriers
- Lack of privacy

Parent-Infant Separation

DEFINITION

Presence of factors that prohibit interaction between infant and parent(s)

DEFINING CHARACTERISTICS

Diagnostic Cues

+ Verbalization by parent(s) indicating fear of interaction (e.g., fear that infant may die, fear of hurting infant)
+ Infrequent contact with infant because of one or more of the following:
  + Inability of parent(s) to visit hospital regularly
  + Absent or limited opportunity for eye-to-eye contact between infant and parent(s)
  + Absent or limited opportunity for tactile interaction
  + Inability of infant to tolerate noise or touch
  + Lack of immediate access to infant

Supporting Cues

+ Verbalization by parent(s) regarding inability to parent the infant because of separation or lack of knowledge about the infant
+ Lack of immediate information regarding infant's condition

ETIOLOGICAL OR RELATED FACTORS

+ Transportation difficulties for family to visit hospitalized infant
+ Support system deficit (e.g., lack of care relief to enable visitation)

HIGH-RISK POPULATIONS

+ Prematurity
+ Critical illness of infant or parent(s)
+ Hospitalization of infant or parent(s)

Readiness for Enhanced Parenting

DEFINITION

Pattern of providing an environment for children or other dependent person(s) that is sufficient to nurture growth and development and can be strengthened

DEFINING CHARACTERISTICS

- Expresses desire to enhance parenting
- Children and other dependent person(s) express satisfaction with home environment
- Evidence of emotional and tacit support of children or dependent person(s)
- Evidence of bonding/attachment
- Meets physical and emotional needs of children/dependent person(s)
- Exhibits realistic expectations of children/dependent person(s)

Caregiver Role Strain

DEFINITION

Caregiver perceives difficulty in performing family caregiver role

DEFINING CHARACTERISTICS

Diagnostic Cues

Caregiver's report of one or more of the following:

+ Inadequate resources to provide required care
+ Difficulty completing required caregiving activities
+ Worry about the care receiver (e.g., care receiver's health and emotional state, having to put the care receiver in an institution, and/or who will care for the care receiver if something should happen to the caregiver)
+ Feeling that caregiving interferes with other important roles in caregiver's life
+ Feeling of loss because the care receiver is "like a different person" compared with before caregiving began
+ In the case of a child, feeling of loss that the care receiver was not the child the caregiver expected
+ Family conflict around issues of providing care
+ Stress or nervousness in caregiver's relationship with the care receiver
+ Depression
+ Dysfunctional change in caregiving activities
+ Preoccupation with caregiving routine

Continues

Caregiver Role Strain—*cont'd*

Supporting Cues
Caregiver Physical Status

+ GI upset (mild stomach cramps, vomiting, diarrhea, recurrent gastric ulcer episodes)
+ Weight change
+ Rash
+ Hypertension, cardiovascular disease
+ Diabetes
+ Fatigue, headaches

Caregiver Emotional Status

+ Impaired coping; lack of time to meet personal needs
+ Disturbed sleep
+ Anger, stress response
+ Somatization
+ Increased nervousness
+ Emotionally labile
+ Impatience, frustration

Caregiver Socioeconomic Status

+ Withdraws from social life
+ Changes in leisure activities
+ Refuses career advancement

Caregiver–Care Receiver Relationship

+ Grief/uncertainty regarding changed relationship with care receiver
+ Difficulty watching care receiver go through the illness
+ Family conflict
+ Concerns about family members

ETIOLOGICAL OR RELATED FACTORS

Pathophysiological/Physiological Factors

- Illness severity, unpredictable course of illness, unstable health (care receiver)
- Caregiver health impairment
- Addiction or codependency
- Discharge of family member with significant home care needs

Developmental Factors

- Caregiver not developmentally ready for caregiver role (e.g., young adult needing to provide care for a middle-aged parent)
- Developmental delay or retardation (care receiver or caregiver)

Psychosocial Factors

- Psychological or cognitive problems (care receiver)
- Deviant or bizarre behavior (care receiver)
- Marginal family adaptation or dysfunction (before caregiving situation)
- Marginal coping patterns (caregiver)

Situational Factors

- Family or caregiver isolation
- Presence of abuse or violence
- Situational family stressors (e.g., significant loss, disaster or crisis; poverty or economic vulnerability; major life events: birth, death, hospitalization, leaving/returning home, marriage, divorce, employment changes, retirement)
- Duration of caregiving

Continues

Caregiver Role Strain—*cont'd*

- Inadequate physical environment for providing care (e.g., housing, transportation, community services, equipment)
- Lack of respite or recreation (caregiver)
- Inexperience with caregiving
- Competing role commitments (caregiver)
- Complexity or amount of caregiving tasks

HIGH-RISK POPULATIONS

- Premature birth or congenital defect
- Significant home care needs
- Female caregiver; caregiver is spouse
- Family stress
- History of poor relationship (caregiver–care receiver)

Risk for Caregiver Role Strain

DEFINITION

Caregiver is vulnerable for perceived difficulty in performing
the family caregiver role

RISK FACTORS

Pathophysiological Risk Factors

- Illness severity, unpredictable course of illness,
  unstable health (care receiver)
- Caregiver health impairment
- Addiction or codependency
- Premature birth or congenital defect
- Discharge of family member with significant home
  care needs
- Caregiver is female

Developmental Risk Factors

- Caregiver not developmentally ready for caregiver role
  (e.g., young adult needing to provide care for middle-
  aged parent)
- Developmental delay or retardation (care receiver or
  caregiver)

Psychological Risk Factors

- Psychological or cognitive problems (care receiver)
- Marginal family adaptation/dysfunction (before the
  caregiving situation)
- Marginal coping patterns (caregiver)
- History of poor relationship (caregiver–care receiver)
- Caregiver is spouse
- Deviant or bizarre behavior (care receiver)

Continues

Risk for Caregiver Role Strain—*cont'd*

Situational Risk Factors

- Family or caregiver isolation
- Presence of abuse or violence
- Situational family stressors (specify; e.g., significant loss, disaster or crisis, poverty or economic vulnerability; major life events: birth, death, hospitalization, leaving or returning home, marriage, divorce, employment changes, retirement)
- Duration of caregiving
- Inadequate physical environment for providing care (e.g., housing, transportation, community services, equipment)
- Lack of respite or recreation (caregiver)
- Inexperience with caregiving
- Competing role commitments (caregiver)
- Complexity or amount of caregiving tasks

Impaired Verbal Communication

DEFINITION

Reduced or absent ability to use language in human interaction

DEFINING CHARACTERISTICS

Diagnostic Cues

- Difficulty expressing thoughts verbally (stuttering, slurring, trouble forming words or sentences) or unable to speak

and/or

- Reports difficulty understanding speech communications

Supporting Cues

- Inappropriate verbalization
- Dyspnea
- Unable to speak dominant language*

ETIOLOGICAL OR RELATED FACTORS

- Psychological barrier (psychosis, lack of stimuli)
- Developmental or age related

HIGH-RISK POPULATIONS

- Physical barrier (brain tumor, tracheostomy, intubation)
- Cultural difference*
- Anatomical defects (cleft palate)
- Decrease in circulation to brain

---

*May not indicate a nursing diagnosis—possibly a care delivery problem requiring a translator or establishing some means of nonverbal communication.

Readiness for Enhanced Communication

DEFINITION

Pattern of exchanging information and ideas with others is sufficient for meetings needs and life goals and can be strengthened

DEFINING CHARACTERISTICS

- Expresses willingness to enhance communication
- Able to speak or write a language
- Forms words, phrases, and language
- Expresses thoughts and feelings
- Uses and interprets nonverbal cues appropriately
- Expresses satisfaction with ability to share information and ideas with others

Developmental Delay: Communication Skills (Specify Type)

DEFINITION

Demonstrates deviations from age-group norms in development of communication skills (specify type of skill)

DEFINING CHARACTERISTICS

Diagnostic Cues

+ Delay or difficulty in performing expressive, communication skills typical of age group or developmental level (e.g., prelanguage vocalization, language skills, signs)

Supporting Cues

+ Flat affect
+ Listlessness
+ Decreased responses

ETIOLOGICAL OR RELATED FACTORS

+ Environmental or stimulation deficiencies
+ Inconsistent responsiveness
+ Multiple caregivers, inadequate caregiving
+ Separation (from significant others)
+ Physical disability effects
+ Prescribed dependence
+ Indifference

327

Risk for Other-Directed Violence

DEFINITION

Behaviors in which an individual demonstrates that he or she can be physically, emotionally, and/or sexually harmful to others

RISK FACTORS

- Body language (rigid posture, clenching of fists and jaw, hyperactivity, pacing, breathlessness, threatening stances)
- History of violence against others (e.g., hitting someone, kicking someone, spitting, scratching, biting, throwing objects at someone, rape or attempted rape, sexual molestation, urinating/defecating on a person)
- History of violence or threats (e.g., verbal threats against property or person, social threats, cursing, threatening notes or letters, threatening gestures, sexual threats)
- History of violent antisocial behavior (e.g., stealing, incessant borrowing, incessant demands for privileges, frequent interruption of meetings, refusal to eat, refusal to take medication, ignoring instructions)
- History of indirect violence (tearing off clothes, ripping objects off walls, writing on walls, urinating on floor, defecating on floor, stamping feet, having temper tantrums, running in corridors, yelling, throwing objects, breaking windows, slamming doors, making sexual advances)
- Other factors (neurological impairment, e.g., positive EEG, CAT, or MRI; head trauma, positive neurological findings, seizure disorders)

ROLE-RELATIONSHIP PATTERN

- Cognitive impairment (e.g., learning disabilities, attention deficit disorder, decreased intellectual functioning)
- History of childhood abuse
- History of witnessing family violence
- Cruelty to animals, fire setting
- Prenatal and perinatal complications/abnormalities
- History of drug and/or alcohol abuse, pathological intoxication
- Psychotic symptomatology (e.g., auditory, visual, command hallucinations; paranoid delusions; loose, rambling or illogical thought processes)
- Motor vehicle offenses (e.g., frequent traffic violations, use of a motor vehicle to release anger)
- Suicidal behavior; impulsivity; availability or possession of weapon(s)

NOTES

NOTES

NOTES

Sexuality-
Reproductive Pattern

Ineffective Sexuality Patterns

DEFINITION

Expression of concern regarding own sexuality

DEFINING CHARACTERISTICS

- Reported difficulties, limitations, or changes in sexual behaviors or activities

ETIOLOGICAL OR RELATED FACTORS

- Knowledge or skill deficit (alternative responses to health-related transitions)
- Altered body function or structure
- Illness or medical treatment
- Lack of privacy
- Lack of significant other
- Ineffective or absent role models
- Conflicts with sexual orientation or variant preferences
- Fear (pregnancy)
- Impaired relationship with significant other

Sexual Dysfunction

DEFINITION

Change in sexual function is viewed as unsatisfying, unrewarding, inadequate

DEFINING CHARACTERISTICS

- Verbalizations of problem in sexual relationships
- Alterations in achieving perceived sex role
- Actual or perceived limitation imposed by disease and/or therapy
- Conflicts involving values
- Alteration in achieving sexual satisfaction
- Inability to achieve desired sexual satisfaction
- Frequent seeking of confirmation of desirability
- Alteration in relationship with significant other
- Change of interest in self and others

ETIOLOGICAL OR RELATED FACTORS

- Ineffectual or absent models
- Physical abuse
- Psychosocial abuse (e.g., harmful relationships)
- Vulnerability
- Misinformation or lack of knowledge
- Values conflict
- Lack of privacy
- Lack of significant other

HIGH-RISK POPULATIONS

- Altered body structure or function (pregnancy, recent childbirth, drugs, surgery, anomalies, disease process, trauma, radiation)

335

Rape Trauma Syndrome*

DEFINITION

Sustained maladaptive response to a forced, violent sexual penetration against the victim's will and consent

DEFINING CHARACTERISTICS

Diagnostic Cues

Acute Phase

+ Report of forced, violent, sexual penetration and one or more of the following:
  + Confusion
  + Disorganization, mood swings
  + Anxiety, agitation, aggression
  + Nightmares or sleep disturbance
  + Disassociative disorders, denial, depression
  + Shock, anger, shame, guilt
  + Humiliation, embarrassment, self-blame
  + Feelings of vulnerability, hyperalertness
  + Helplessness, powerlessness
  + Inability to make decisions
  + Dependence
  + Fear of physical violence and death
  + Muscle tension or spasms, gastrointestinal irritability
  + Physical trauma (bruising, tissue irritation), genitourinary discomfort
  + Paranoia
  + Loss of self-esteem

---

*This syndrome includes the following three subcomponents: Rape Trauma, Compound Reaction, and Silent Reaction. In this text each appears as a separate diagnosis.

SEXUALITY-REPRODUCTIVE PATTERN

Long Term

- Changes in lifestyle, changes in residence
- Suicide attempts
- Phobias, substance abuse
- Sexual dysfunction
- Change in relationships
- Nightmares or sleep disturbance

Rape Trauma Syndrome: Compound Reaction

DEFINITION

Forced, violent sexual penetration against the victim's will and consent. The trauma syndrome that develops from this attack or attempted attack includes an acute phase of disorganization of the victim's lifestyle and a long-term process of reorganization of lifestyle

DEFINING CHARACTERISTICS

Diagnostic Cues

See defining characteristics listed under Rape Trauma Syndrome.

- ◆ Reactivated symptoms of previous conditions (i.e., physical illness, psychiatric illness)
- ◆ Reliance on alcohol and/or drugs

Rape Trauma Syndrome: Silent Reaction

DEFINITION

Presence of signs and symptoms but without victim's mentioning to anyone that rape has occurred

DEFINING CHARACTERISTICS

Diagnostic Cues

See defining characteristics listed under Rape Trauma Syndrome.

- No initial verbalization of the occurrence of rape
- Abrupt changes in relationships with men
- Increase in nightmares
- Increasing anxiety during interview (blocking of associations, long periods of silence, minor stuttering, physical distress)
- Marked changes in sexual behavior with opposite sex
- Sudden onset of phobic reactions

NOTES

NOTES

NOTES

Coping–Stress-Tolerance Pattern

Ineffective Coping (Specify)*

DEFINITION

Impairment of adaptive behaviors (valid appraisal, choice of response, and/or inability to use resources). Methods of handling stressful life situations are insufficient to prevent or control anxiety, fear, or anger. Specify stressor(s) (e.g., situational or maturational crises, uncertainty)

DEFINING CHARACTERISTICS

Diagnostic Cues

- Reports presence of life stress or problems (specify)
- Reports feeling anxious, apprehensive, fearful, angry, and/or depressed
- Expresses inability to cope or ask for help
- Ineffective or inappropriate use of defense mechanisms (forms of coping that impede adaptive behavior, e.g., see avoidance coping, denial)

Supporting Cues

- Disturbance in pattern of tension release
- Disturbance in pattern of threat appraisal
- Inadequate resources (financial, etc.)
- Change in usual communication patterns
- Decrease in use of social support
- Poor concentration
- Lack of goal-directed behavior and resolution of problem (e.g., inability to attend to problem; difficulty organizing information)
- Inability to meet role expectations
- Inability to meet basic needs
- Destructive behavior toward self or others

---

*There may be gender differences in coping strategies.

- Sleep disturbance
- Fatigue
- Risk taking
- High illness rate
- Abuse of chemical agents
- High degree of perceived or actual threat

ETIOLOGICAL OR RELATED FACTORS

- Inadequate problem solving
- Inadequate confidence in coping ability
- Inadequate perception of control
- Social support deficit or characteristics of relationships
- Inability to conserve adaptive energies

HIGH-RISK POPULATIONS

- Inadequate opportunity to prepare for stressor

Readiness for Enhanced Coping

DEFINITION

Pattern of cognitive and behavioral efforts to manage demands that is sufficient for well-being and can be strengthened

DEFINING CHARACTERISTICS

- Defines stressors as manageable
- Seeks social support
- Uses a broad range of problem-oriented and emotion-oriented strategies
- Uses spiritual resources
- Acknowledges power
- Seeks knowledge of new strategies
- Is aware of possible environmental changes

Avoidance Coping*

DEFINITION
Prolonged minimization or denial of information (facts, meanings, consequences) when a situation requires active coping

DEFINING CHARACTERISTICS
Diagnostic Cues
- Presence of perceived threat to health, self-image, values, lifestyle, or relationships
- Minimizes, ignores, or forgets information following clear communication or observation
- Mislabels events
- Absence of problem solving, information seeking, incorporation of new information into future planning

Supporting Cues
- Regressive dependency
- Anxiety, depression, passivity, or anger

ETIOLOGICAL OR RELATED FACTORS
- Perceived incompetency
- Perceived powerlessness
- Support system deficit
- Independence-dependence conflict (adolescent)

---

*Avoidance is not to be confused with hope or adaptive denial. See also Denial.

347

Defensive Coping

DEFINITION

Repeated projection of falsely positive self-evaluation based on a self-protective pattern that defends against underlying perceived threats to positive self-regard

DEFINING CHARACTERISTICS

Diagnostic Cues

One or more of the following:

- Denial of obvious problems or weaknesses
- Projection of blame or responsibility
- Rationalization of failures
- Hypersensitivity to a slight or a criticism
- Grandiosity

Supporting Cues

- Superior attitude toward others
- Difficulty establishing or maintaining relationships
- Hostile laughter or ridicule of others
- Difficulty in reality testing of perceptions
- Lack of follow-through or participation in treatment or therapy

ETIOLOGICAL OR RELATED FACTORS

- Perceived threat to self (specify)

Ineffective Denial or Denial*

DEFINITION

Conscious or unconscious attempt to reduce anxiety or fear by disavowing the knowledge or meaning of an event (to the detriment of health)

DEFINING CHARACTERISTICS

Diagnostic Cues

- Unable to admit impact of disease or event on life pattern as manifested by one or more of the following:
- Delays seeking or refuses health care to the detriment of health; does not admit fear of death or invalidism; displaces fear of impact of the condition; unrealistic plans
- Selectively integrates information
- Does not perceive danger or personal relevance of symptoms; minimizes symptoms or event

Supporting Cues

- Makes dismissive gestures or comments when speaking of distressing events
- Displaces source of symptoms to other organs
- Inconsistent expression of fear or anxiety
- Displays inappropriate affect
- Uses home remedies (e.g., self-treatment) to relieve symptoms

*It is unclear whether the adjective ineffective before the word denial relates to the diagnosis or its consequences. It is not consistent with definition and characteristics specified. Suggestion: use "Denial or Partial Denial," or see Avoidance Coping. Caution must be exercised in attempting to treat this condition (help the patient to fully recognize a threat or danger) during a crisis situation (e.g., surgery, infarct).

Risk for Suicide

DEFINITION
Presence of risk factors for self-inflicted, life-threatening injury

RISK FACTORS
+ Behavioral
+ History of prior suicide attempt
+ Impulsiveness
+ Buying a gun
+ Stockpiling medicines
+ Making or changing a will
+ Giving away possessions
+ Sudden euphoric recovery from major depression
+ Marked changes in behavior, attitude, school performance

Verbal
+ Threats of killing oneself
+ States desire to die/"end it all"

Situational
+ Living alone
+ Retired
+ Relocation, institutionalization
+ Economic instability
+ Loss of autonomy/independence
+ Presence of gun in the home
+ Adolescents living in nontraditional settings (e.g., juvenile detention center, prison, half-way house, group home)

COPING–STRESS-TOLERANCE PATTERN

Psychological

- Family history of suicide
- Alcohol and substance use/abuse
- Psychiatric illness/disorder (c.g., depression, schizophrenia, bipolar disorder)
- Abuse in childhood
- Guilt
- Gay or lesbian youth

Demographic

- Age: Elderly, young adult, males, adolescents
- Race: Caucasian, Native American
- Gender: Male
- Marital Status: Divorced, widowed

Physical

- Physical illness, terminal illness
- Chronic pain

Social

- Loss of important relationship
- Disrupted family life
- Grief, bereavement
- Support system deficit
- Loneliness
- Hopelessness, helplessness
- Social isolation
- Legal or disciplinary problem
- Cluster suicides

Compromised Family Coping

DEFINITION

Usually supportive primary person (family member or close friend) providing insufficient, ineffective, or compromised support, comfort, assistance, or encouragement, which may be needed by client to manage or master adaptive tasks related to health challenge

DEFINING CHARACTERISTICS

Diagnostic Cues

+ Client or another person expresses concern or complaint about significant other's response to client's health problem

and one or more of the following:

+ Significant person displays protective behavior disproportionate (too little or too much) to client's abilities or need for autonomy
+ Significant person describes preoccupation with personal reactions (e.g., fear, guilt, anticipatory grief, anxiety) to client's illness, disability, or other situational or developmental crises
+ Significant person describes or confirms inadequate understanding of knowledge base that interferes with effective assistive or supportive behaviors (specify)
+ Significant person withdraws or enters into limited or temporary personal communication with client at time of need
+ Significant person attempts assistive or supportive behaviors with less than satisfactory results

COPING–STRESS-TOLERANCE PATTERN

ETIOLOGICAL OR RELATED FACTORS

- Knowledge deficit (specify area)
- Emotional conflicts (specify)
- Exhaustion of supportive capacity (see Caregiver Role Strain)
- Role changes (family)
- Temporary family disorganization
- Developmental or situational crises (specify)

HIGH-RISK POPULATIONS

- 24-hour home care
- Home care with periodic health crises
- History of family life stresses

Disabled Family Coping

DEFINITION

Behavior of significant person (family member or primary person) disables own capacities and client's capacities to effectively address tasks essential to either person's adaptation to the health challenge

DEFINING CHARACTERISTICS

Diagnostic Cues

+ Neglectful care of client in regard to basic human needs and/or illness treatment

and one or more of the following:

+ Distortion of reality regarding client's health problem, including extreme denial about existence or severity (see also Denial)
+ Intolerance
+ Rejection
+ Abandonment
+ Desertion
+ Carrying on usual routines, disregarding client's needs
+ Psychosomaticism
+ Taking on illness signs of the client
+ Decisions and actions by family that are detrimental to economic or social well-being
+ Agitation, depression, aggression, hostility
+ Impaired restructuring of a meaningful life for self, impaired individuation, prolonged overconcern for client
+ Neglectful relationships with other family members
+ Client's development of helpless, inactive dependence

COPING–STRESS-TOLERANCE PATTERN

ETIOLOGICAL OR RELATED FACTORS

+ Chronically unexpressed guilt, anxiety, hostility by significant other
+ Dissonant discrepancy of coping styles (for dealing with adaptive tasks by the significant person and client or among significant people)
+ Highly ambivalent family relationships
+ Arbitrary handling of family's resistance to treatment (tends to solidify defensiveness as it fails to deal adequately with underlying anxiety)

HIGH-RISK POPULATIONS

+ 24-hour home care
+ History of family life stresses
+ Home care with periodic health crises

Readiness for Enhanced Family Coping

DEFINITION

Effective management of adaptive tasks involved with the client's health challenge by family member, who now exhibits desire and readiness for enhanced health and growth in regard to self and in relation to the client

DEFINING CHARACTERISTICS

- Family member moves in direction of health-promoting and enriching lifestyle that supports and monitors maturational processes, audits and negotiates treatment programs, generally chooses experiences that optimize wellness
- Individual expresses interest in making contact on a one-to-one basis or on a mutual-aid group basis with another person who has experienced a similar situation
- Family member attempts to describe growth impact of crisis on own values, priorities, goals, or relationships

Ineffective Community Coping

DEFINITION

Pattern of community activities for problem solving that is unsatisfactory for meeting the demands or needs of the community

DEFINING CHARACTERISTICS

- Community does not meet its own expectations
- Deficits in community participation
- Excessive community conflicts
- Expressed vulnerability
- Expressed community powerlessness
- High illness rates
- Stressors perceived as excessive
- Increased social problems (e.g., homicides, vandalism, arson, terrorism, robbery, infanticide, abuse, divorce, unemployment, poverty, militancy, mental illness)

ETIOLOGICAL OR RELATED FACTORS

- Community social support deficit
- Inadequate resources for problem solving
- Ineffective or nonexistent community systems (e.g., lack of emergency medical system, transportation systems, disaster planning systems)

HIGH-RISK POPULATIONS

- Natural or man-made disasters

Readiness for Enhanced Community Coping

DEFINITION

Pattern of community activities for adaptation and problem solving that is satisfactory for meeting the demands or needs of the community but can be improved for management of current and future problems or stressors

DEFINING CHARACTERISTICS

- Deficits in one or more characteristics that indicate effective coping
- Active planning by community for predicted stressors
- Active problem solving by community when faced with issues
- Agreement that community is responsible for stress management
- Positive communication among community members
- Positive communication between community and/or aggregates and larger community
- Programs available for recreation and relaxation
- Resources sufficient for managing stressors

ETIOLOGICAL OR RELATED FACTORS

- Social supports available
- Resources available for problem solving
- Community has a sense of power to manage stressors

COPING–STRESS-TOLERANCE PATTERN

Support System Deficit*

DEFINITION

Insufficient emotional and/or instrumental help from others

DEFINING CHARACTERISTICS

One or more of the following:

- Lack of one or more persons who communicates positive regard about personal worth and competence
- Insufficient or absent social network to provide instrumental assistance (e.g., transportation, household tasks)
- Lack or unavailability of a confidant

Supporting Cues

- Absence of visitors
- Reports feeling anxious or apprehensive
- Reports feeling depressed
- Disorganized behavior
- Reports somatic complaints
- Irritable or hostile

HIGH-RISK POPULATIONS

- Elderly lacking family and experiencing death of friends
- Small or absent social network

*This condition is frequently a focus for intervention (i.e., etiological/related factors).

Impaired Adjustment

DEFINITION

Inability to modify lifestyle or behavior in a manner consistent with a change in health status

DEFINING CHARACTERISTICS

- ◆ Disability or health status change requiring change in lifestyle
- ◆ Failure to take actions that would prevent further health problems
- ◆ Demonstration of nonacceptance of health status change
- ◆ Failure to achieve optimal sense of control

ETIOLOGICAL OR RELATED FACTORS

- ◆ Denial of health status change
- ◆ Absence of social support for changed beliefs and practices
- ◆ Multiple stressors
- ◆ Lack of motivation to change behaviors
- ◆ Intense emotional states
- ◆ Negative attitudes toward suggested healthy behavior
- ◆ Low state of optimism
- ◆ Failure to intend to change behavior

Post-Trauma Syndrome

DEFINITION

Sustained maladaptive response to a traumatic overwhelming event

DEFINING CHARACTERISTICS

Reaction

- Intrusive thoughts
- Detachment
- Psychogenic amnesia
- Hypervigilance
- Substance abuse
- Compulsive behavior
- Avoidance, alienation
- Shame, guilt
- Grief, hopelessness
- Denial, repression

Emotional/Cognitive

- Sadness, depression
- Anxiety, fear
- Horror
- Anger, rage, aggression
- Irritability
- Panic attacks
- Difficulty in concentrating
- Flashbacks, exaggerated startle response

Physical

- Gastric irritability
- Neurosensory irritability, palpitations
- Headaches
- Enuresis (in children)   *Continues*

Post-Trauma Syndrome—*cont'd*

Sleep

+ Intrusive dreams
+ Nightmares

HIGH-RISK POPULATIONS

+ Events outside the range of usual human experience:
  + Natural or manmade disasters
  + Witnessing mutilation, violent death, or other horrors
  + Sudden destruction of one's home or community
  + Tragic occurrence involving multiple deaths
  + War or military combat
  + Serious threat or injury to self or loved ones
  + Held prisoner of war or criminal victimization (torture)
  + Serious industrial and motor vehicle accidents
  + Physical and psychological abuse

Risk for Post-Trauma Syndrome

DEFINITION

Risk for sustained maladaptive response to a traumatic overwhelming event

RISK FACTORS

- Non-supportive environment
- Inadequate social support
- Survivor's role in the event
- Exaggerated sense of responsibility
- Perception of event
- Duration of event
- Occupation (police, fire, rescue, corrections, emergency room staff, mental health provider)
- Displacement from home
- Diminished ego strength

Self-Mutilation

DEFINITION

Deliberate self-injurious behavior causing tissue damage with the intent of causing nonfatal injury to attain relief of tension

DEFINING CHARACTERISTICS

- ◆ History of self-injurious behavior
- ◆ Cuts/scratches on body
- ◆ Picking at wounds
- ◆ Self-inflicted burns (e.g., eraser, cigarette)
- ◆ Ingestion/inhalation of harmful substances/objects
- ◆ Biting; abrading; severing; hitting; constricting a body part
- ◆ Insertion of object(s) into body orifice(s)

RELATED FACTORS

- ◆ Adolescence; fluctuating emotions
- ◆ Childhood illness or surgery, foster, group, or institutional care
- ◆ Incarceration
- ◆ Isolation from peers
- ◆ Perfectionism
- ◆ Low or unstable body image
- ◆ Command hallucinations; sexual identity crisis
- ◆ History of inability to plan solutions or see long-term consequences
- ◆ Dysfunctional family (violence between parental figures; family alcoholism/divorce/history of self-destructive behavior)
- ◆ Use of manipulation to obtain nurturing relationship with others
- ◆ Chaotic/disturbed interpersonal relationships
- ◆ Childhood sexual abuse; substance abuse; eating disorder

- Emotionally disturbed and/or battered children
- Feels threatened with actual or potential loss of significant relationship (e.g., loss of parent or parental relationships)
- Experiences dissociation or depersonalization; character disorders; borderline personality disorders
- Feelings of depression, rejection, self hatred, separation anxiety, guilt and depersonalization

HIGH-RISK POPULATIONS

- Borderline personality disorder, especially females 16 to 25 years of age
- Psychotic state; frequently males in young adulthood
- Emotionally disturbed and/or battered children
- Mentally retarded and autistic children
- History of self-injury or history of physical, emotional, or sexual abuse

Risk for Self-Mutilation

DEFINITION

Presence of risk factors for deliberate self-injurious behavior causing tissue damage with the intent of causing nonfatal injury to attain relief of tension

RISK FACTORS

- Inability to cope with increased psychological or physiological tension in a healthy manner
- Experiences mounting tension that is intolerable
- Impulsivity
- Inability to express tension verbally; experiences irresistible urge to cut/damage self
- Needs quick reduction of stress
- Rationalizations or rejections of positive feedback
- Feelings of depression, rejection, self-hatred, separation anxiety, guilt, depersonalization
- Peers who self-mutilate
- Adolescence; fluctuating emotions
- Childhood illness or surgery, foster, group, or institutional care
- Incarceration
- Isolation from peers
- Perfectionism
- Low or unstable body image
- Command hallucinations; sexual identity crisis
- History of inability to plan solutions or see long-term consequences
- Need for sensory stimuli
- Parental emotional deprivation
- Dysfunctional family (violence between parental figures; family alcoholism/divorce/history of self-destructive behavior)

COPING–STRESS-TOLERANCE PATTERN

- Use of manipulation to obtain nurturing relationship with others
- Chaotic/disturbed interpersonal relationships
- Childhood sexual abuse; substance abuse; eating disorder
- Emotionally disturbed and/or battered children
- Feels threatened with actual or potential loss of significant relationship
- Loss of parent or parental relationships
- Experiences dissociation or depersonalization; character disorders; borderline personality disorders
- Loss of control over problem-solving situations
- Developmental delay or autism
- History of self-injurious behavior
- Feelings of depression, rejection, self hatred, separation anxiety, guilt and depersonalization

NOTES

NOTES

NOTES

Value-Belief Pattern

VALUE-BELIEF PATTERN

Spiritual Distress

DEFINITION

Impaired ability to experience and integrate meaning and purpose in life through a connectedness with self, others, art, music, literature, or a power greater than oneself

DEFINING CHARACTERISTICS

Connections to Self

♦ Expresses lack of one or more of the following: hope, meaning and purpose in life, peace/serenity, acceptance, love, forgiveness of self, courage
♦ Anger
♦ Guilt
♦ Poor coping

Connections with Others

♦ Refuses interactions with spiritual leaders
♦ Refuses interactions with friends, family
♦ Verbalizes being separated from support system
♦ Expresses alienation

Connection with Art, Music, Literature, Nature

♦ Inability to express previous state of creativity (singing, listening to music, writing)
♦ No interest in nature
♦ No interest in reading spiritual literature

Connections with Power Greater Than Self

♦ Inability to pray
♦ Inability to participate in religious activities
♦ Expresses being abandoned by or having anger toward God

VALUE-BELIEF PATTERN

- Inability to experience transcendence
- Request to see a religious leader
- Sudden changes in spiritual practices
- Inability to be introspective or inward turning
- Expresses being without hope, suffering

ETIOLOGICAL OR RELATED FACTORS

- Self-alienation
- Loneliness
- Social alienation
- Anxiety
- Sociocultural deprivation
- Death and dying of self or others
- Pain
- Life change
- Chronic illness of self or others

Risk for Spiritual Distress

DEFINITION
Presence of risk factors for an impaired ability to experience and integrate meaning and purpose in life through connectedness with self, other persons, art, music, literature, nature, and/or a power greater than oneself

RISK FACTORS
Physical

- Physical illness
- Substance abuse/excessive drinking
- Chronic illness

Psychosocial

- Low self-esteem
- Depression
- Stress/anxiety
- Poor relationships
- Separated from support systems
- Blocks to experiencing love
- Inability to forgive
- Loss
- Racial/cultural conflict
- Change in religious rituals or spiritual practices

Developmental

- Life change

Environmental

- Environmental changes
- Natural disasters

Readiness for Enhanced Spiritual Well-Being

DEFINITION

Ability to experience and integrate meaning and purpose in life through connectedness with self, others, art, music, literature, nature, or a power greater than oneself

DEFINING CHARACTERISTICS

Connections to Self

- Desire for enhanced hope, meaning and purpose in life, peace, serenity, acceptance, surrender, love, forgiveness of self, satisfying philosophy of life, joy, courage
- Heightened coping
- Meditation

Connections with Others

- Provides service to others
- Requests interactions with spiritual leaders
- Requests forgiveness of others
- Requests interactions with friends, family

Connections with Art, Music, Literature, Nature

- Displays creative energy (writing, poetry)
- Sings, listens to music
- Reads spiritual literature
- Spends time outdoors

Connections with Power Greater Than Self

- Prays
- Reports mystical experience
- Participates in religious activities
- Expresses reverence, awe

Impaired Religiosity

DEFINITION

Impaired ability to rely on beliefs and/or participate in rituals of a particular faith tradition

DEFINING CHARACTERISTICS

- ◆ Demonstrates or expresses difficulty adhering to prescribed religious beliefs and rituals (e.g., religious ceremonies, dietary regulations, clothing, prayer, worship/religious services, private religious behaviors/reading religious materials/media, holiday observances, meeting with religious leaders)
- ◆ Expresses need to reconnect with previous belief patterns and customs
- ◆ Expresses emotional distress because of separation from faith community
- ◆ Questions religious belief patterns and customs*
- ◆ Expresses emotional distress regarding religious beliefs and/or religious social network*

ETIOLOGICAL OR RELATED FACTORS

- ◆ Pain/suffering
- ◆ Ineffective coping (e.g., with disease)
- ◆ Deficient support system
- ◆ Lack of security
- ◆ Anxiety
- ◆ Fear of death
- ◆ Cultural barriers (to practicing religion)
- ◆ Environmental barriers (to practicing religion)
- ◆ Lack of social integration
- ◆ Lack of social/cultural interaction
- ◆ Spiritual distress (spiritual crisis)
- ◆ Use of religion to manipulate

*See Spiritual Distress.

HIGH-RISK POPULATIONS

- End-stage life crises
- Aging
- Sickness/illness
- Personal disaster/crisis
- Life transitions

Risk for Impaired Religiosity

DEFINITION

Presence of risk factors for impaired ability to rely on religious beliefs and/or participate in rituals of a particular faith tradition

RISK FACTORS

- Illness/hospitalization
- Pain
- Suffering
- Ineffective coping
- Deficient support system
- Depression
- Lack of security
- Lack of social interaction
- Cultural barriers to practicing religion
- Environmental barriers to practicing religion
- Social isolation
- Lack of transportation
- Life transitions

Readiness for Enhanced Religiosity

DEFINITION

Desire/ability to increase reliance on religious beliefs and/or participate in rituals of a particular faith community

DEFINING CHARACTERISTICS

- Expresses desire to strengthen religious belief patterns and customs that have provided comfort/religion in the past
- Request for assistance to increase participation in prescribed religious beliefs through religious ceremonies, dietary regulations/rituals, clothing, prayer, worship/religious services, private religious behaviors/reading religious materials/media, holiday observances
- Requests assistance expanding religious options
- Requests meeting with religious leaders/facilitators
- Requests forgiveness, reconciliation
- Requests religious material and/or experiences
- Questions or rejects belief patterns and customs that are harmful

NOTES

NOTES

NOTES

Glossary

GLOSSARY

Approved nursing diagnoses   Health-related conditions submitted by nurses that have been reviewed and accepted as nursing diagnoses by NANDA International; (2) classes or categories of health problems in a nursing diagnostic classification system.

Assessment   The collection and interpretation of clinical data; (2) a health-status evaluation done by a health professional.

Defining characteristic   An observable sign, verbal report, or contextual attribute that increases the probability of a diagnosis; (2) serves as a cue or indicator of a diagnosis; (3) a sign or symptom; (4) a historical or current indicator of client-environment interaction; (5) a human response.

Diagnostic cue   An observable sign, verbal report, or contextual attribute that serves as a critical indicator of a health problem; a specific criterion that strongly influences the probability of a diagnosis; (2) a sign or symptom that is usually present when a specific diagnosis is present; (3) a defining characteristic.

Documentation   Recording of observations, judgments, actions, test results, events, and plans related to the health or health care of an individual, family, or community; (2) may be entries in a computer or on paper documents.

Etiological factors   Probable causes of a health problem; (2) usually research-based, causal relationships.

Functional health pattern   A configuration (interrelated information) of health-related behaviors that occurs sequentially across time; (2) sequences of health-related behaviors; (3) a specific division in a typology.

High-risk population   Individuals, families, or groups that have a greater than average risk for a condition described by a nursing diagnosis.

North American Nursing Diagnosis Association   (Name changed to NANDA International in 2004) An organization of American and Canadian nurses and nurses from other countries dedicated to the identification, development, and classification of nursing diagnoses.

Nursing diagnosis "A clinical judgment about individual, family, or community responses to actual or potential health problems/life processes. Nursing diagnoses provide the basis for selection of nursing interventions to achieve outcomes for which the nurse is accountable" (NANDA International); a name for an actual or potential health problem or life process that refers to a set of human responses; a specific class or category in a diagnostic classification system.

Related factors Conditions or events having some association with a health problem.

Risk factor An observable sign, verbal report, or contextual attribute that is an indicator of a potential problem or risk state.

Supporting cue An observable sign, verbal report, or contextual attribute that serves as an indicator of more than one health problem; (2) information that influences confidence in a diagnostic judgment; (3) a sign or symptom; (4) a defining characteristic, usually of one or more diagnoses.

Taxonomy A set of rules and procedures for classification; (2) also used to refer to the classification system that is organized by the rules or procedures.

Index

INDEX

Continued from first page